BEADING
In No Time

50 step-by-step designs for beautiful bead jewelry

linda peterson

CICO BOOKS

LONDON NEW YORK

Published in 2010 by CICO Books

An imprint of Ryland Peters & Small Ltd

20–21 Jockey's Fields   519 Broadway, 5th Floor

London WC1R 4BW   New York NY 10012

www.cicobooks.com

10 9 8 7 6 5 4 3 2

ISBN-13: 978 1 907030 26 0

Printed in China

Editor: Marie Clayton

Designer: David Fordham

Photographer: Geoff Dann, Emma Mitchell, and David Munns

contents

introduction

I was born to create; I can't help it! The creative bug runs rampant in my family—both of my grandmothers loved to sew, my mother quilts and paints china, and my aunts are into just about every creative thing imaginable. However, it's my Aunt June who inspired me with my love of beading and jewelry making.

The shapes, the colors, the textures: there is something alluring about beads. Have you ever gone up to a bowl of them and immersed your hands to feel the textures and the shapes, letting them roll off your fingertips? Beads are amazingly therapeutic.

Beading and beadwork is nothing new, far from it! Did you know that beads have been around for thousands of years? In many places and times they were used as currency, and were worn by those of elite social status. Why, just look at portraits of the late Queen Victoria in all her glory, decked out in waterfalls of beads!

As I've come to write this book, I've discovered that beads are a personal reflection of you, of your style. They give the onlooker a glimpse into your personality. And not only that, beaded fashions can make an ordinary outfit into an extraordinary one. Your beading skills do not have to be extraordinary, nor do you have to be a wealthy queen to create really beautiful pieces. With the techniques outlined in this book, creating beautiful jewelry is right at your fingertips.

If you are a first-time beader, there are a couple of things I must warn you about. First of all, after your first beading experience everything you look at will become inspiration—the colors, the shapes, the textures all around you will take on new meaning. Secondly, after all the oohs and ahhs from your friends, you will quickly find yourself addicted. You won't be able to create just one piece: you'll have to create the whole ensemble.

The projects in this book are arranged roughly in order of difficulty, so the first chapter, Simply Stated, was planned with first-time and busy beaders in mind. The projects here take less than an hour to create, so you can literally create and wear your jewelry on the go. Fabulous Focals has projects with focal pendants that are a little more complex to make. In Multi-strand Designs, we create designs with multiple strands, some of which are fairly simple in design but will take a little longer just because there are so many elements to make. The final chapter, Bead Weaving and Wire Wrapping, introduces the ancient technique of peyote bead weaving, but also includes some beautiful projects where silver wire is twisted artistically with beads to create truly unique designs.

As you become more acquainted with beading and the techniques, try your hand at mixing and matching—perhaps you like the design of one piece, for instance, but would prefer it in the colors used in another design. This will open up a whole new world of combinations and possibilities and your creative spirit will take over.

So now, there's only one question to ask: what are you waiting for? Get lost in the creative spirit and get beading!

linda peterson

tools, materials, and techniques

It's my goal to make your first beading experience a very pleasant one. In order to do that, it is best to have the appropriate tools for the job. These don't have to cost you a fortune, but you will find that quality tools and materials will help to make your beading experience that little bit easier and much more enjoyable.

tools and materials

cutting and shaping tools

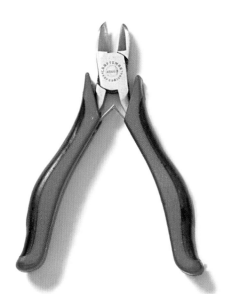

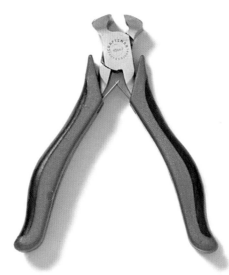

Standard pliers:

Basic pliers useful for bending wire. These particular pliers have no serrated edge, so they will not leave any marks on wire, jump rings, or other findings.

Standard wire cutters:

Useful when cutting wire—note that some wire cutters tend to cut wire into a sharp point.

Flush cutters:

Wire cutters that cut "flush," meaning flat with no point at the end of the length of wire.

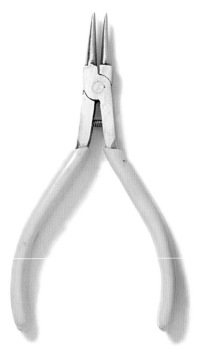

Round-nose pliers:

Useful when creating loops at the end of wires or when creating coils as a decorative element.

Crimping pliers (blue handle and white handle):

These are used with crimp beads to secure the bead to beading wire. They come in a variety of sizes depending on the size of the crimp bead used.

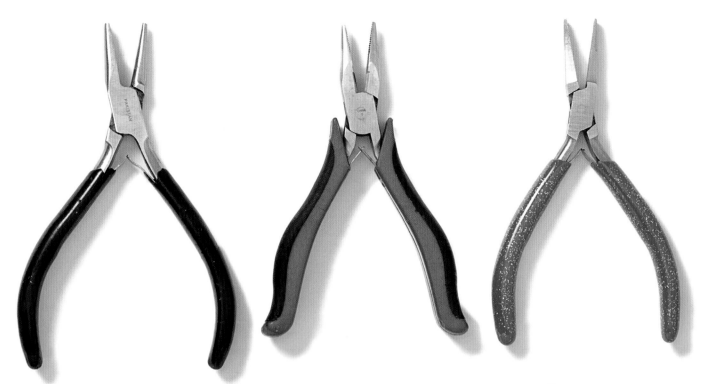

Bail-making pliers:

These are useful when creating wire bails or bending decorative elements to create a bail. I also use them to make jump rings, or to create a loop at the end of the wire. Bail-making pliers are one of my favorite and most versatile tools.

Basic pliers with serrated edges:

The serrated edges on these pliers mean they have a really tight grip. Be careful when using them, though, because they can leave little marks on your findings.

Flat-nose pliers:

These have squared edges and are useful to create sharp angles. They are also handy when making coils because they keep the coils flat, and they may also be used to straighten bent wire.

general tools

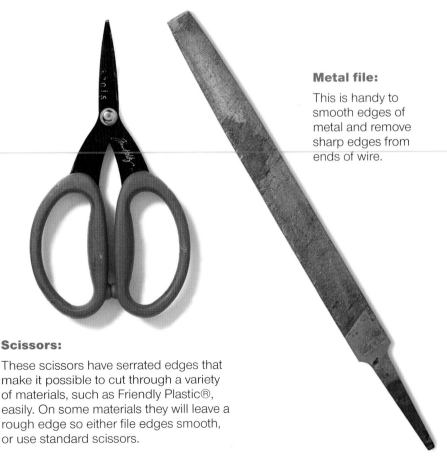

Metal file:

This is handy to smooth edges of metal and remove sharp edges from ends of wire.

Hole punch:

To create a small hole in projects, so that jump rings can be attached.

Scissors:

These scissors have serrated edges that make it possible to cut through a variety of materials, such as Friendly Plastic®, easily. On some materials they will leave a rough edge so either file edges smooth, or use standard scissors.

general tools

Ring mandrel:
Useful for sizing and creating rings.

Rubber stamp:
This one happens to come with four different stamps on a long handle. However, any deeply etched, simple design of your choice will work.

Bead reamer:
Used to enlarge, de-burr, and round out bead holes, making the beads easier to string.

Wooden stylus:
Used as a base to create jump rings, mix resin, or create patterns in metal.

Needle tool:
Used to marble designs in Friendly Plastic®.

Hand drill:
For drilling holes in resin focal pieces.

Other materials:

Dowel rods:
These are available in a variety of widths.

Inkpad:
Standard black ink pad.

Heat gun:
Standard heat gun used in several of our projects to dry stamping ink and to melt Friendly Plastic®.

chains and stringing materials

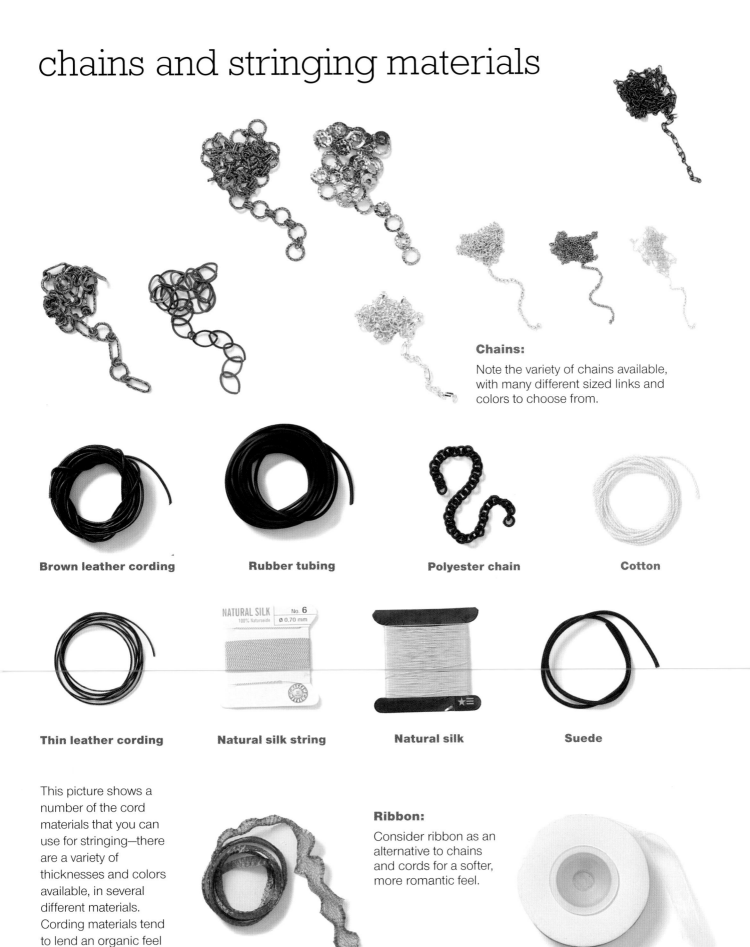

Chains:
Note the variety of chains available, with many different sized links and colors to choose from.

Brown leather cording

Rubber tubing

Polyester chain

Cotton

Thin leather cording

NATURAL SILK No. 6
100% Naturseide Ø 0.70 mm

Natural silk string

Natural silk

Suede

This picture shows a number of the cord materials that you can use for stringing—there are a variety of thicknesses and colors available, in several different materials. Cording materials tend to lend an organic feel to your jewelry.

Ribbon:
Consider ribbon as an alternative to chains and cords for a softer, more romantic feel.

stringing tools and materials

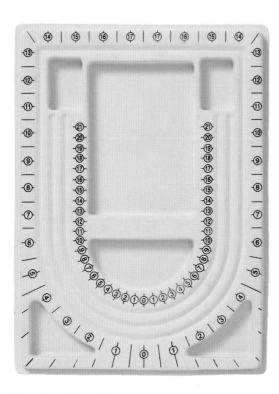

Beading board:

Useful when designing stringing patterns, especially when you are working with multiple-strand designs. It will give you an idea of what the finished design will look like, so that you can make changes before stringing.

Beading needles:

These are used with Wildfire™ bead string thread and are helpful when creating complex designs with small beads, such as in the peyote stitch.

Seed bead spinner:

This is an excellent tool to string seed beads onto bead thread quickly and easily. A real time saver!

Other materials:

Wildfire™ bead stringing thread:

This is specially designed to be used with seed beads and other beads with smaller holes. It resists fraying and stretching.

Elastic cording:

This stretches and is handy when making bracelets because you don't have to worry too much about sizing.

Bead stringing wire:

This is suitable for most jewelry projects because it is durable and comes in a variety of thicknesses.

Supplemax:

An ideal choice for creating illusion and floating designs. Perfect for stringing plastic, wood, and other non-abrasive beads.

Bead stringing wire in colors:

The colors available range from silver and gold to reds, blues, and greens. It can be used as a decorative element in your jewelry fashions.

Stretch magic:

Another brand of elastic cording, which also comes in various widths.

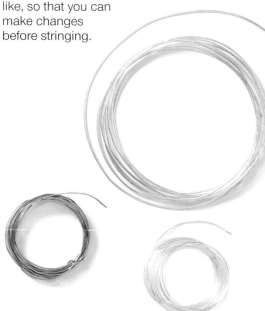

Wire:

This comes in a variety of colors and gauges. My favorite is silver non-tarnish wire, which is a silver-coated copper wire that stays bright like sterling silver but is inexpensive.

adhesives, resin, and Friendly Plastic®

Friendly Plastic®:
This is a decorative plastic that melts at low temperature and comes in strips in a variety of colors and patterns. It is great to add extra interest when making focal pendants.

Glue:

E-6000 is a silicone-based glue useful for attaching filigree components together. Diamond Glaze is another alternative, though not silicone based. Both glues dry clear and need to be used with proper ventilation.

Casting resins:

These are two-part and can be poured into molds to create focal pendants. A variety of mixed media, such as glitter, can be added to give stunning results.

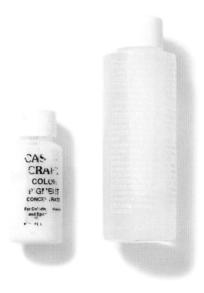

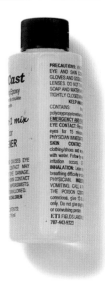

findings

Crimp beads and ends:

A variety of crimping beads and ends are used, depending on the type of stringing material. They also come in a variety of sizes and finishes.

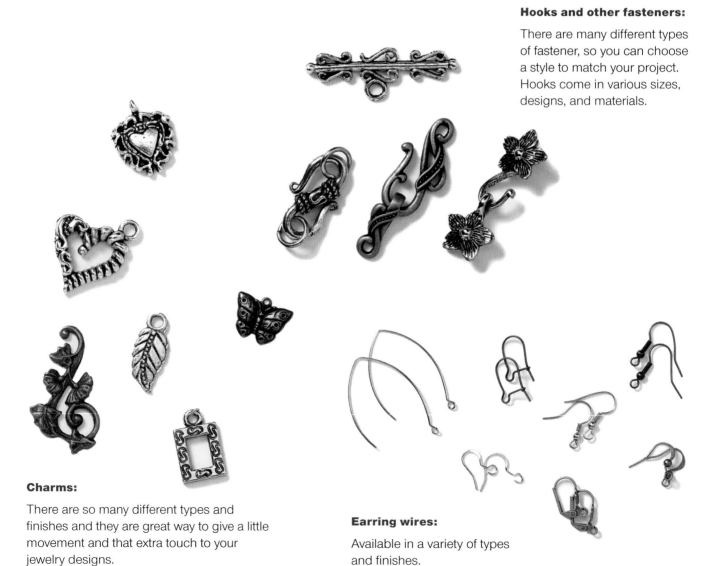

Hooks and other fasteners:

There are many different types of fastener, so you can choose a style to match your project. Hooks come in various sizes, designs, and materials.

Charms:

There are so many different types and finishes and they are great way to give a little movement and that extra touch to your jewelry designs.

Earring wires:

Available in a variety of types and finishes.

Ends:

There are many different findings that can be used to give a finished look to your multi-strand pieces. Decorative cones can combine multi-strands into one strand.

Toggles and lobster clasps:

These are available in many shapes, sizes and designs. Toggles may also be used as a focal point in your design to achieve a unique effect.

Filigree findings:

These add a decorative touch to your pieces. Other embellishments and crystals can be added to them, giving them an extra touch of sparkle.

Miscellaneous findings:

Key rings, large lobster clasps that can be used for handbag charms or zipper pulls, and cell phone (mobile) charms. Using these, you can quickly make hanging pieces of many different types.

findings

Other materials:

Rub-N-Buff®:

Metallic wax finishes that can be used to change the color of findings or to give them a vintage antique look.

tip

Broken jewelry that cannot be repaired—or items that have gone out of fashion or you don't like anymore—can be taken apart and the components reused. Odd lengths of chain are particularly useful, and this is a great way to recycle and save money.

Links:

These often have a little loop at the top and bottom, and can be used as decorative elements in your designs. Available in a variety of shapes, sizes, and finishes.

Jump rings:

Available in a variety of sizes, shapes, and finishes, or you can easily make your own using wire—see page 25 for the technique.

Head pins and eye pins:

Head pins come with flat heads or decorative elements at the base of the pin. Eye pins have a loop at one end. Both are available in several finishes.

beads

Glass beads:

These come in a variety of shapes and sizes; some are smooth and others are faceted. Swarovski™ crystals will add a real touch of sparkle, but Czech glass beads are more affordable and will create a very similar effect.

Seed beads:

These come in a variety of sizes and many different colors. They can be used as spacer beads as well as for the peyote stitch.

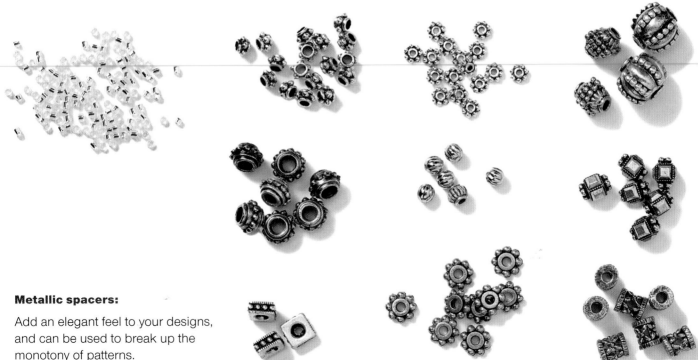

Metallic spacers:

Add an elegant feel to your designs, and can be used to break up the monotony of patterns.

beads

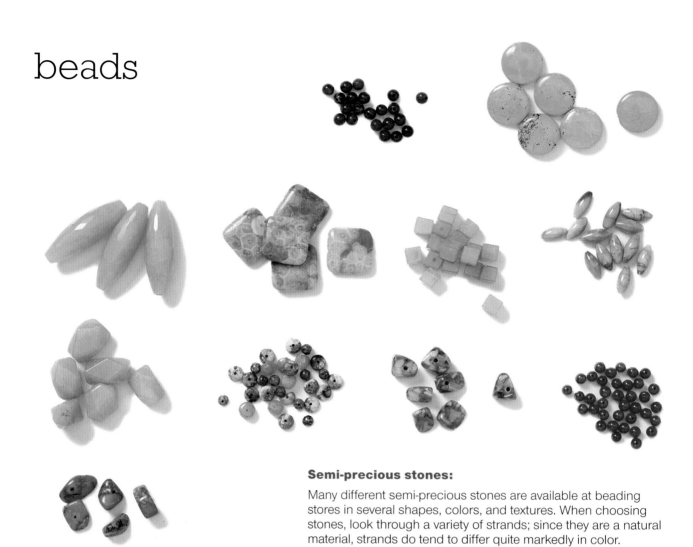

Semi-precious stones:

Many different semi-precious stones are available at beading stores in several shapes, colors, and textures. When choosing stones, look through a variety of strands; since they are a natural material, strands do tend to differ quite markedly in color.

Wooden beads:

To lend an organic or ethnic look to your designs.

techniques

using a crimp bead

A crimp bead is used to attach a finding—usually a jump ring—to the end of a length of bead stringing wire, and also to hold individual beads in position and prevent them sliding to the end.

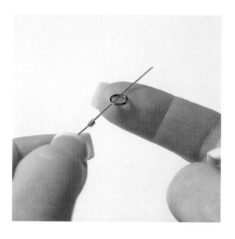

1 String a crimp bead onto bead stringing wire and add a jump ring.

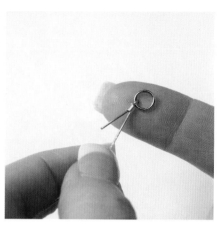

2 Fold the wire over the jump ring and back through the crimp bead. Pull the loop tight against the jump ring.

3 Using crimping pliers, squeeze the crimp bead down firmly against the beading wire.

4 Trim the end of the wire to approximately ½in. (12mm), but no less than ¼in. (6mm) to prevent the end from pulling back through the jump ring and allowing all your beads to come off.

5 String beads over both wires to cover the end of the beading wire. Continue stringing beads until your design is complete. To finish a project using a crimp bead, repeat steps 1 and 2. Thread the end of the wire back through the last few beads, pull the loop tight, and crimp the bead with pliers. Trim off any excess wire with wire cutters.

using the beading board

The beading board has several grooves that can be used to lay out different lines of beads. It is not only useful for designing your stringing layout, but will also keep the beads neatly in order until you are ready for them.

1 Use the beading board to lay out your stringing design. A beading board is especially helpful when a specific length is important or when making a multi-strand piece of jewelry. It saves time in the long run because it allows you to get an idea of what the piece will look like before you begin stringing.

making jump rings

Jump rings are one of the basic components that you will use time and again. There are many sizes and shapes available, but it is also very easy to make your own.

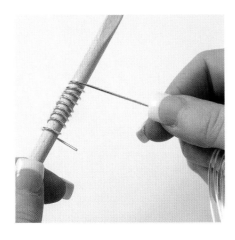

1 Wind the wire around a length of dowel rod or any other object of the desired width (circumference).

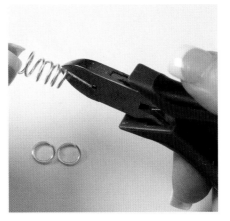

2 Slide the wire spiral off the rod and snip the coils into separate rings with wire cutters.

tip

Jump rings do not have to be round; add interest to your designs by making square or triangular jump rings.

opening and closing jump rings

Use this simple method to open and close jump rings so you can thread items onto them.

tip

Don't open a jump ring by pulling the ends apart, as this will distort the shape and it will be hard to get it back into a perfect circle. By opening them in the way shown here, they stay perfectly round.

1 To open a jump ring, hold a pair of pliers on each side of the slit and twist the pliers slightly in opposite directions, opening up a gap.

2 To close the ring, repeat the twisting action in reverse to bring the ends back together neatly.

changing the color of findings

Findings come in a basic range of colors, but if you want something different you can easily make changes with colored resin or different metallic waxes.

1 Colored resin can be applied directly to many metal findings to change the color. Special effects can also be added to make them sparkle, such as adding glitter.

2 When you need a gold finding but only have silver, you can change the color by simply rubbing a little metallic wax over the top of the finding and letting it dry. To permanently seal it, go over with any clear varnish or clear nail polish.

creating dangles on head pins

Many of the designs in this book have dangles, which you can easily make yourself. Using your own dangles, rather than purchased ones, will give your jewelry its own unique look.

1 Thread a bead onto a head pin.

2 Add smaller beads and spacers to make the design of your choice. Trim the excess wire to around ¼–½in. (6–12mm) in length.

3 Curve the top of the head pin into a loop, then cut off any excess wire. Attach the loop to your jewelry design as desired.

tip

When making a symmetrical necklace design, make the center dangle and then make the others in pairs to be sure that they will match.

creating beaded links with eye pins

Links between different sections of a design do not have to be plain chain—you can make decorative links with beads of your choice. These can be any length you need; just make a loop at each end so that they can be joined.

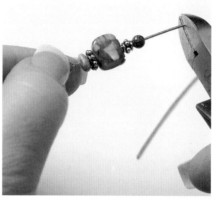

1 Cut a length of wire. Using round-nose pliers, bend the end into a small ring. You may also use an eye pin instead.

2 Thread beads onto the wire to create the desired pattern. Snip off the excess wire, leaving ¼–½in. (6–12mm) remaining.

3 Using round-nose pliers, curve the wire to create a loop at the end as close in size as possible to the one made in step 1.

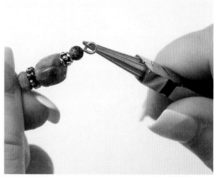

4 Adjust the two rings as necessary, so that they are both centered on the line of the wire.

creating an S-clasp and hook

Making the S-clasp

If you want to try making your own clasp, this design is very simple and easy. The S-clasp can be used with a jump ring, or see the hook on page 30.

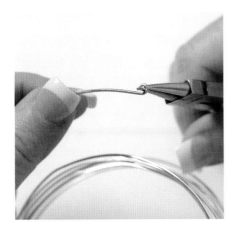

1 Cut a piece of wire approximately 4in. (10cm) long and create a loop at one end with round-nose pliers.

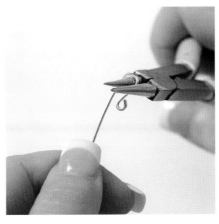

2 Bend the wire backward around the round-nose pliers.

3 Bend the wire back on itself again in the opposite direction.

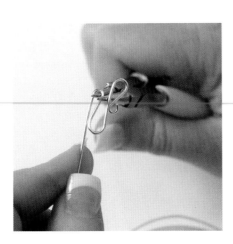

4 Bend it again in the first direction to create the "S" shape.

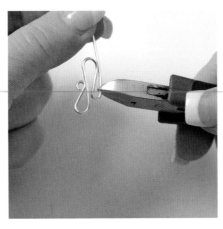

5 Snip off the excess wire and finish with a loop.

6 Flatten the clasp on an anvil, if necessary.

Making the hook

This hook is very sturdy and can be used on its own to catch into one of the links in a length of chain, or with the S-clasp on page 29. You can make it to the size you need, so it's very versatile.

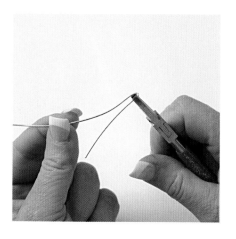

7 Cut a piece of wire approximately 4in. (10cm) long. Using the flat-nosed pliers, fold it in two, leaving one end longer than the other.

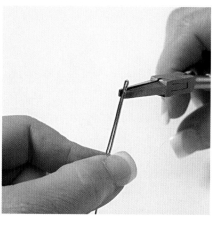

8 Pinch the ends together with pliers.

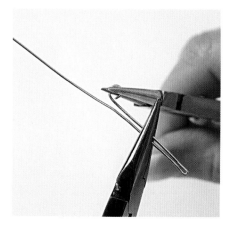

9 Form the short end into a loop.

10 Wrap the long end above the loop several times to secure, and trim off any excess wire.

11 Bend the doubled end around the round-nose pliers to create a hook.

12 Curve the end of the hook back again slightly to create an upturned tip.

working with resin

Resin is ideal to make focal pendants to any shape and size. You will need a selection of shaped molds, but these can be used time and again. Resin is clear, but can easily be colored.

tip

If you want to add motifs to your resin, see the technique in Flower Power on page 51.

1 Pour equal amounts of hardener and resin into a clean container. Stir with a popsicle (lolly) stick for 3 minutes until well mixed.

2 Pour the mixed resin carefully into the mold.

3 Scatter glitter, mica flakes, or other decorative bits over the surface of the resin and gently stir in. Put aside to set for at least 12 hours—timing may vary with the local temperature.

4 When the resin is set, flex the mold slightly, while pushing on the shape to pop it out.

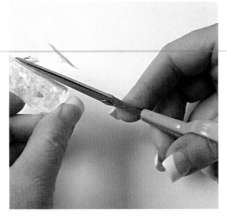

5 Clean up any roughness around the edges by trimming the excess with scissors.

6 Smooth the edges by filing, if necessary. Use a small hand drill to drill a small hole right through the shape for hanging, if required.

creating focal pieces with Friendly Plastic®

Drawing designs

Friendly Plastic® comes in many colors and patterns as standard, but if you want something a little different you can draw your own design with oil-based paint. Set the design by applying a little heat.

1 Cut a piece of Friendly Plastic® and place it on a heat-resistant baking sheet. Dab some oil-based paint over the surface with the tip of your finger.

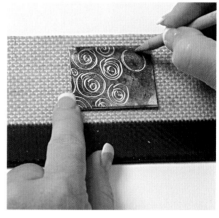

2 Draw your chosen design into the paint, using a point such as a stylus or toothpick.

Combining pieces to create new patterns

Another way of creating something unique is to cut small pieces of Friendly Plastic® and melt them into one another to make a new design. The plastic will melt at quite a low heat.

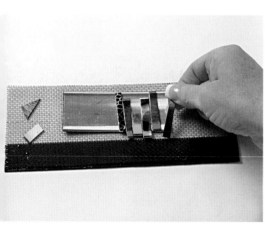

1 Cut a piece of Friendly Plastic® and add narrow strips of different designs and colors on top.

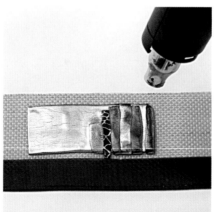

2 Heat up the plastic gently with a heat gun until all the layers become very soft and flexible.

3 Draw lines across the sheet with the tip of a stylus to pull the colors and patterns into random designs and shapes.

Cutting shapes

When it is heated a little, Friendly Plastic® quickly becomes soft and very flexible. At this point it is easy to cut—even with a simple cookie-cutter. This means it is easy to create your own shapes.

1. Heat up a piece of Friendly Plastic® gently with a heat gun until the sheet becomes soft and flexible.

2. Cut out the required shape with a cookie cutter.

3. To support the plastic shape, add it to a metal backing piece using some silicone glue.

tip

If you place your piece of Friendly Plastic® on a heat-resistant sheet right from the start, you can move it around by moving the sheet instead of having to pick it up with your fingers. This means you don't risk marking the paint finish when drawing the design, or getting ready to heat.

beading knots

Basic square macramé knot This decorative macramé knotting technique is based on creating simple square (reef) knots using multiple strands of cord. To keep track of which strands you are using, you could mark them at one end.

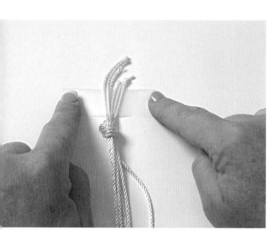

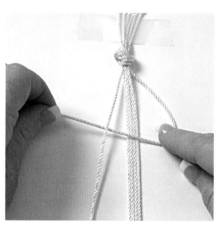

1 Knot six cords together at the top, then tape the cords above the knot down to a hard surface.

2 Lay the cords out flat, running toward you in a straight line. Take the far right cord and lay it over the middle cords. Place it under the left-hand cord, holding it in place on the right with your finger.

3 Take the left-hand cord under the middle cords and thread it through the loop in the right-hand cord, holding it in place on the left with your finger.

tip

You can add beads to your knotted design by threading them on as you work, just as in traditional macramé designs.

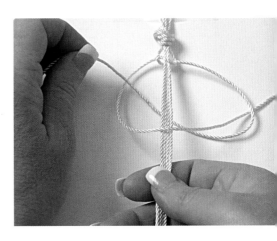

4 Pull on the two cords evenly to bring the knot you have just made gently up under the original knot. This completes half of the square knot.

5 Take the left-hand cord over the middle cords and under the right-hand cord, holding it in place on the left with your finger.

6 Take the right-hand cord under the middle cords and thread it through the loop in the left-hand cord, holding the middle cords in place.

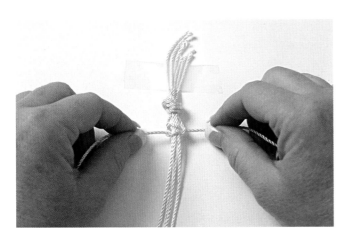

7 Pull on the two cords evenly to bring the knot you have just made gently up under the original knot. This will complete one entire square knot sequence.

Beading knot

Beading knots are used to hold individual beads in place on a length of cord, but can also be used decoratively, as seen on these lengths of leather cord.

1 Knots can be used to hold beads in place on cord, just as crimp beads are used on wire. Thread the bead onto the cord, then make a loose knot in the cord. Work the knot into the right position next to the bead before tightening it.

basic peyote stitch

Peyote stitch is a way of creating a beaded "fabric" that can be used in jewelry making in several different ways. It looks complex, but is actually quite simple to do.

1 Thread a bead onto string and double knot.

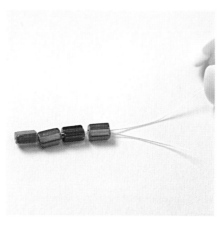

2 Begin threading tube beads onto the string, one at a time. Note how the beads are being threaded over the end as well; this helps hide the extra string.

3 Keep adding beads until you have the desired length, ensuring that there is an even number of beads. Now working on the next row, thread a bead onto the needle, skip over the first bead, and thread the needle through the second bead.

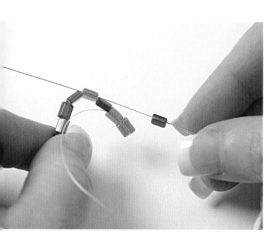

4 Thread another bead on the needle, skip over the third bead, place the needle into the fourth bead, and pull. Continue in this pattern, adding a bead, skipping one bead, and threading through the next. As you begin the third row, you will notice that beads are beginning to form an interlocking pattern.

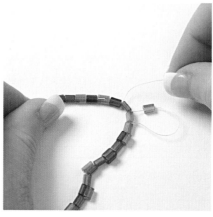

5 Keep working back and forward in this same way, until you have several rows of interlocking beads in the desired width and length.

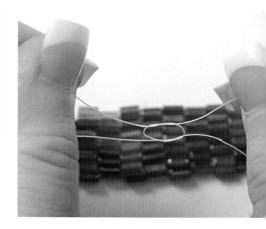

6 If you run out of thread before you finish your beading, tie on a new length using a simple square (reef) knot and pull tight. Weave the loose ends into the beading as you continue to work.

designing jewelry

Everybody wants to look their best most of the time, and it's also natural that we tend to wear what we like and what we feel most comfortable in. But consider for just a minute how selecting the right jewelry for your fashion style and individual taste reflects on your confidence level, self-esteem, and overall mood.

How do you feel when your hair and make-up are perfect and you are dressed to the hilt; you are ready to take on what the day will bring. For me, this is empowering! It lifts my self-esteem and confidence level to the "I can do anything I set my mind to do today" mood. In contrast, if I wear no makeup and put on my most comfy clothes, my mood goes from "I can do anything" to "...okay maybe I'll do something" and I'm much less likely to accomplish all that I set out to do.

The way you present yourself, including the accessories you choose, also says a lot about you—especially to others. I'm not saying in the least that designing jewelry has to be difficult or that you have to put this huge thought process into it every time, but here are some ideas that you might float around in your head while you are in the creative process.

A style of jewelry to fit the occasion

If you were attending a very formal wedding, funky, wild jewelry would probably not go very well with a classic, sophisticated dress. Perhaps that is rather a drastic

example, but you get the idea: a formal event requires sophisticated and classic-style jewelry. On the other hand, you wouldn't want to wear tiny, discreet items of jewelry with a colorful and extravagant outfit—on this occasion, it would be more appropriate to have big, bold accessories. So: fit the style of jewelry to the occasion.

Deciding what suits you

As I mentioned before, you will feel more comfortable if you wear what you like. Personally I wear mostly my own handmade jewelry: it's bold, sometimes rather chunky, and it's out there—but then again, that's who I am. So now let's talk about creating jewelry that suits who you are. Stop reading for a second and go get a mirror. Hold it up and take a good look at yourself in the mirror; get up close and personal. Pull your hair back and concentrate on the shape of your face. Let's talk about these different facial shapes and how jewelry can compliment them to make you look your very best. A rule of thumb is to select necklines and accessories that are the opposite of your facial shape.

Here are just a few of the most common:

Oval or oblong shaped faces are longer than they are wide. While they look very similar overall, if you were to place them side by side, you would be able to see the difference; the oval has soft, rounded curves all round while the oblong is rounded but more angular. Almost any shape of neckline will be flattering to these shape faces, and you have the most options when choosing necklace lengths. You also have the widest choice of jewelry styles, but try adding contrast to an oval shape by wearing angular shapes—and with an oblong face, chokers look especially well.

Round faces have an equal distance all around the face, with the nose being the center point of measure. This shape is wide with rounded edges, so it is important to add some visual length. Scoop, square, v-neck, or mock turtlenecks are most complimentary necklines, but stay away from anything that will add visual thickness to your neck. When it comes to jewelry, choose a longer necklace length and earrings that are oblong or rectangular to create balance.

Heart-shaped faces are wider at the eye line and narrow down to the chin, usually with soft lines and curves. Scoop and boat-shape necklines work well, but avoid anything that ends in a point, such as a V-neck. To balance this shape with jewelry, consider earrings that are the direct opposite, such as triangles that are pointed at the top and wide at the bottom. Chokers, U-shape, or multi-strand necklaces will soften and minimize the point of the chin.

Square or rectangular facial shapes are very similar, with straight lines at the forehead and down the sides, and a square-shape chin. The rectangular face is slightly elongated and narrower, but both of these shapes have strong, defined lines. Choose necklines such as turtlenecks, jewel necks, or those that hang off the shoulder, to soften the angular effect. With jewelry, shapes that are round and wide are best; consider longer earrings to soften a strong jaw line. If your face is narrower, short dangling earrings can help fill out the sides. With necklaces, try for soft U-shapes and multi-strands to offset pronounced facial features.

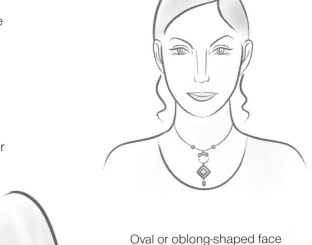

Oval or oblong-shaped face

Round-shaped face

Heart-shaped face

Square or rectangular-shaped face

Match your necklace to the shape of your neckline—the most common mistake is not usually the neckline itself, but a mismatched pairing of neckline and necklace. The focal part of your necklace should be against a flat area of your skin or against the fabric in your outfit—don't have it hidden in your cleavage. With earrings, also remember your hairstyle: don't wear big and bold with short hair, or insignificant earrings with longer hair.

Now let's focus on choosing the right jewelry for a couple of other areas that are fun to accessorize.

Bracelets need to be in proportion to your overall body frame. If you are average to tall, wear wider bracelets, while narrow bracelets are a better choice for petite or small frames. If you have a fuller frame but want to wear narrow bracelets, combine several bands to add balance. Wider bracelets minimize the size of your hands while thin bracelets enhance the size your hands. If you have long arms, steer clear of simple, delicate designs that make your arms look even longer and thinner visually.

Rings should make the best of your hands. If you have long, slender fingers, nearly any style or shape will be flattering. Thin fingers look better with a wider ring band to visually diminish their narrow shape, with an oval or round stones or delicate decoration. If your fingers are thick wear large, oversized rings to draw attention to the ring rather than your fingers and hands. If you have short fingers, a narrow ring band and longer marquise shapes will add visual length and be more flattering.

selling your jewelry

If you're sitting there reading this thinking to yourself, "Seriously... sell my jewelry? Who would buy it?" then you really need to listen to how I started. As I said in the introduction, I've always been creative. But there is a difference between being creative/giving away your work, and being creative/selling your work. The difference is you; it's in how you perceive yourself. Do you see yourself as a seller? I didn't at first, but then here's my story.

Way back in the early 1990s I was always sewing, doing decorative painting, and embellishing clothing. When my second child was born, I switched from embellishing my own clothes to embellishing and making baby clothes. However, when Mariah was about three months old, she became very sick and was diagnosed with a brain tumor. She wound up in the hospital for several months and, in order to keep my sanity, I continued to embellish baby clothes right there in her hospital room. One day, a nurse walked in and asked if I could make something for her to take to a baby shower as a gift. I thought, "Wow, someone actually wants to pay me for what I'm making! What a huge compliment." I thought it was just a one-off, but word spread around the hospital and soon I was making and selling all sorts of things and adding to our income. My business grew into traveling to craft shows, selling wholesale, and finally to the design side of the business.

And to ease your mind about Mariah, she is now 18, cancer free, and creates right along with me. My son Alex is also creative in a different way; he is pursuing a career in architecture. Sometimes I do think about all that I would have missed out on if Mariah had not become sick. Would something else have happened to cause me to sell my work? Perhaps, who knows? What I do know is that I love every minute of it and that it first proved a good way to make some extra income, and is now how I make my living—while still having a great time with my children.

Getting started

So, where to begin. This subject could fill a whole book, but let's focus on the basics. Two things you must have are access to a computer and a camera to take up-close photos. Take some good clear pictures of everything you make and carry these in your handbag as a portfolio, just in case someone asks what you do or if you sell your work. I've even been known to sell the jewelry off my neck! Don't forget to tell everyone you can about your new venture—be a shameless self-promoter.

The next thing is to define your style and your jewelry niche. Where and who is your market? Check out the Internet; if you don't have Internet access yourself, your local library will almost certainly give you free access to it. Try a search on topics such as "how to sell your jewelry" or "how to make money with your art." Believe me, with today's technology you will not be at a loss for information on this subject and you can see what else is out there.

To look professional, you will need business cards. Several online sites will print cards at a reasonable cost, with templates that you can personalize with your contact information. A word of warning: you cannot control whose hands the cards fall into, so if you are working from home, you may wish to omit your address and

handmade items. Setting up your store is free, but there is a minimal charge to place your items up for sale. Etsy also offers a free newsletter filled with excellent tips to promote yourself and your site. Another option is to join message boards/groups with common interests. Yahoo groups are popular and have loads of topics to choose from, or you can start your own. These groups offer a wealth of inspiration, education, and marketing opportunities—and you'll build great friendships, too!

Your own domain name and web page can be costly, but if you are serious about building a business it is worth the investment of time and money. Many web hosting sites allow you to pick a suitable domain name and help you get started with online templates; you simply supply the wording and the photographs.

So now you have an online presence, you need to promote it! Join social networking sites such as **Facebook** and **Twitter**: they can be useful business tools. Think of them as your commercials: manufacturers spend thousands every day to keep their products in the public eye, but you can do the same for free. The more friends and subscribers you have, the more chances to sell your work. It's all about networking, patience, and time.

Link your blog and online store into your social networking sites—there is an abundance of information online on how to do this. When your sites are linked, the information and pictures you post on your blog/store will automatically appear on the social networking sites as well. Subscribers, friends, or followers of your posts will

simply use your email or phone contact. Carry your cards with you at all times, giving them out like candy. Really, trust me, people do like to see what you have to offer; remember that you are providing them with a time-saving service for all their gift-giving needs!

Going online

To reach a wider audience you need an online presence. If you are starting out on a budget like I did, first try blogging about your wares. You do not have to have amazing technical skills; it's as simple as having an email address and a password. There are several services like **Blogger** or **Wordpress** that allow you to create a free online blog; just find one that suits you. A blog is like writing in your journal, but on the web for others to read. Blogging sites are easy to update as often as you like: several times a day, daily, weekly. You can post pictures of your work, and those interested can subscribe to your blog and receive updates to their email box when you write something new.

You can sell from your blog, but if things go well you may want to set up an online store. This is easy with sites such as **Etsy**, a popular online marketplace that features

also receive direct notification when you add something. Be sure to update your blog and online store each time you create something new for sale, when you are offering a special sale, or simply to give your fans fresh ideas that will make them want to make a purchase. Setting all of these online things up takes a lot of extra time and effort, but afterwards they pretty much run themselves, so it's worth taking that time to get them going.

Arts and crafts fairs

Another avenue for selling is to have a presence at arts and crafts shows. Use the Internet to find out about shows coming up in your region or area, and join local artist guilds, which are a great resource of information as well. This avenue of sales will require you to invest some money for displays, tables, and booth/stand rental. These shows are not only for selling; they provide a great opportunity for you to meet prospective clients one-on-one. This will give you an insight into what they are looking for so it will help you to design and cater to a specific local market. It also means that you can develop personal business relationships, which grow over time. It's satisfying to know who is purchasing your work and where it is finding a new home.

If you want to do weekend shows, home party boutiques, or trunk shows consider these tips:

◆ Dress for success—wear your art. Sorry, but don't wear your t-shirt and jeans unless they are in some way artful. This is not the time for your comfy sweatpants, and no matter how tired you are, don't look it: smile!
◆ Create an attractive display that will place the focus on your jewelry, not your props.
◆ Talk and be friendly, even if you know people aren't going to purchase. Just because they don't purchase today doesn't mean they won't in the future. Thank people for stopping by.
◆ Have a guest book with you and ask everyone to sign up for your newsletter or blog using their email address.
◆ Research the show beforehand so you have a good idea what else will be on sale. You need to be aiming for a similar type of market, but try to offer something unique.

◆ Place a business card in with each sale. Get creative with your packaging—it says a lot about who you are—and make sure your contact information is clearly printed on it.

Think positively about yourself and your work at all times. I have done art shows that seemed a real flop at the time, only to get a phone call later from someone who took my card in a hurry and then wanted to place an order. And she told her friend who placed an order too... you see, you're always building relationships. Always wear your own jewelry —you'll be surprised how many people notice it—and guess what? It gives you an opportunity to give out your card. If nothing else, having your work admired just makes your day!

simply
stated

The projects in this chapter will introduce you to beading and jewelry making—they will enable you to create designer items in an hour or less. Although simple and easy to execute, the stunning pieces featured here will really make a statement and add a touch of elegance to your wardrobe.

basic ring

These rings are entirely handmade without using any purchased jewelry findings, but they are so quick to do that you could easily make several as unique presents and really impress your friends. The ring section is made from simple loops of silver wire and can be made to fit any size finger.

1 Thread an 8in. (20cm) length of wire through one of the beads and twist the ends around the stone.

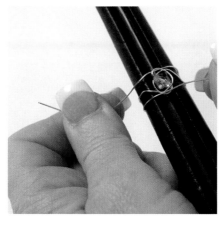

2 Place the stone into the groove on the back of the ring mandrel at the right size level and wrap the ends of the wire around the mandrel a couple of times.

estimated time to complete

Less than an hour

materials

20- or 26-gauge (0.8 or 0.4mm) wire, depending on bead size

4mm, 6mm, or 8mm faceted beads

tools

Ring mandrel

Wire cutters

Pliers

Metal file

3 Take the ring off the mandrel and twist one end of the wire around the main part of the ring, close to the stone on one side.

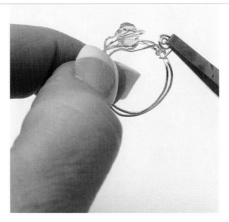

4 Coil the end of the wire to add a decorative element. Press the coil against the side of the ring with pliers. Repeat steps 3–4 on the other side.

tip
Use the gauge of wire that goes best with the size of your stone—the thinner wire with the smaller stones and the thicker wire with the larger ones.

bling bling ring

Estimated time to complete

Less than an hour

materials

20-gauge (0.8mm) wire

26-gauge (0.4mm) wire

Feature bead of choice

tools

Ring mandrel

Wire cutters

Flat-nose pliers

Round-nose pliers

Metal file

If statement pieces are more your style than the rather discreet basic ring on page 47, these Bling Bling Rings are the ones for you. They feature much larger stones, which are held in place with baroque swirls and spirals of silver wire. Choose a stone with a central hole so the wire can be threaded through to hold it firmly in place.

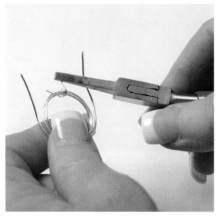

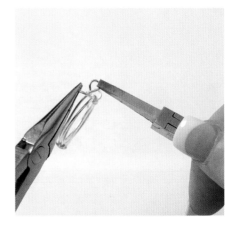

1 Wrap an 8in. (20cm) length of 20-gauge (0.8mm) silver wire around the ring mandrel slightly smaller than the size you wish to make. Leave the two ends protruding on each side.

2 Wrap a short length of 26-gauge (0.4mm) wire around the loops at one point to hold them together neatly.

3 Create a loop with round-nose pliers on the end of each loop and wrap wire end around ring to secure. Trim off any excess wire.

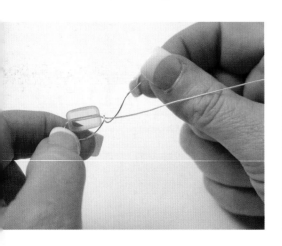

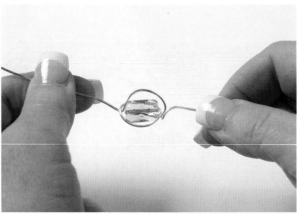

4 Thread a 4in. (10cm) length of 26-gauge (0.4mm) wire through the stone, taking one end over the stone and looping it around the other end.

5 Wind the other end of the wire around the other side of the bead, giving it a decorative touch.

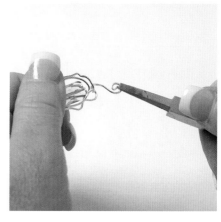

6 Continue winding the wire around the bead, creating random decorative swirls as you do so.

7 Curl the loose end of the wire into a spiral.

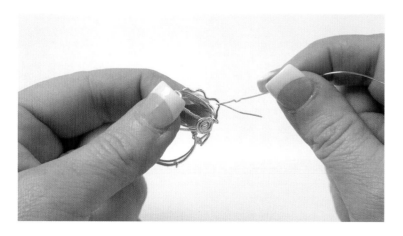

8 Cut a 3in. (7.5cm) piece of 26-gauge (0.4mm) wire. Wrap around a loop on the wrapped bead several times and secure the opposite end to the loop on the ring. Curl and coil any remaining wire, or trim off excess if no additional embellishment is desired.

9 Secure the opposite end of the wire to the loop on the ring.

tip

Make the ring slightly smaller than needed at first. When you place it back on the mandrel to round it out, you can then stretch it to the appropriate size. If you start with the right size, you may enlarge it too much when you are working it back into a round shape in step 11.

10 Curl and coil any remaining wire on this side, or simply trim off excess if desired.

11 Place the ring back onto the ring mandrel and work it gently backward and forward to make sure the ring is a perfect circle.

flower power resin

The pretty flower on the pendant of this necklace is just a sticker included in the resin when it is cast, with a second layer of colored resin added behind so it shows up nicely. Resin is a wonderful material to work with, but allow it to cure for 24 hours before handling.

estimated time to complete

Less than an hour excluding resin curing time

materials

Two-part clear resin

Glitter

Transparency with image or use a sticker

White colorant

Bead stringing wire

2 pink faceted 8mm beads

2 white glass 10mm beads

4 crimp beads

4 jump rings

Lobster clasp

tools

Jewelry mold

Scissors

Sandpaper or fine file

Hand drill

Wire cutters

Crimp pliers

1 Follow manufacturer's directions for mixing equal amounts of the resin and hardener. Add a little glitter and then stir consistently for three minutes, trying to add as few air bubbles as possible.

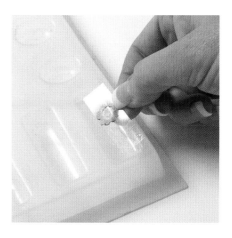

2 Pour the mixed resin carefully into the mold. Cut the transparent image to fit the mold and place it on top of the liquid resin.

3 Add a second layer of white colored resin to seal the image within the shape, but do not fill to the top of the mold. Place the resin in its mold aside to set for at least 12 hours.

4 When the first layer is set, mix up more resin and add one drop of white colorant. Pour this onto the back of the shape to fill the mold. Allow to cure. When set, carefully push the shape out of the mold.

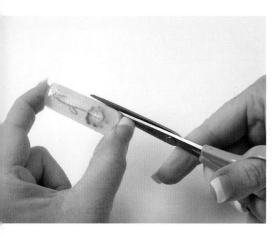

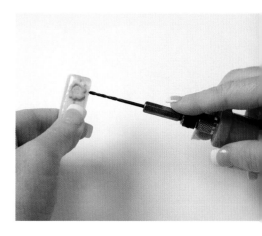

5 Trim any rough edges off neatly with scissors.

6 Smooth the edges with a piece of fine sandpaper or a fine file.

7 Use a hand drill to drill a small hole right through the top of the shape for the wire to be threaded for hanging.

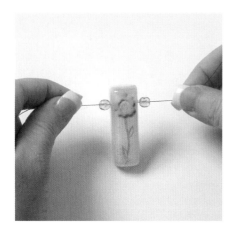

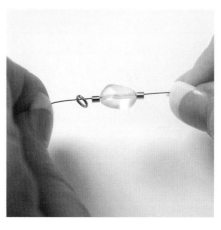

8 Thread a length of bead stringing wire through the hole in the shape. Add a faceted bead on either side of the central shape.

9 Thread on a crimp bead, glass bead, crimp bead, and jump ring at one end of the bead stringing wire.

10 Place the end of the bead stringing wire over a jump ring and back through to the last crimp. Pull tight to secure, leaving a ¼in. (5mm) end protruding from the last crimp. Flatten the crimp with crimp pliers as described on page 24. Trim excess wire. Repeat steps 9–10 at the other end of the wire. Attach a clasp with jump rings.

tip

When working with resin you will need to leave it for at least 12 hours to cure. If you are pouring several layers—to enclose something within the resin, or to add different layers of color—you may need to allow a little more time.

pretty in pink necklace

This zingy pink heart was made with an ordinary silver heart charm and a little touch of glittery resin. Here it is hung on a simple chain, but you could also use it as one of many charms on a more complex necklace—or in place of the charm used in Heartfelt on page 76 or the Spirals Keychain on page 60.

estimated time to complete

Less than an hour excluding resin curing time

materials

Two-part resin	1 head pin
Alcohol ink color of choice	1 small jewel charm
Glitter	Bead cap
Silver heart charm	Length of delicate chain
1 flat-back crystal	3 jump rings
6mm and 8mm beads	Lobster clasp

tools

Mixing pot	Tweezers
Toothpick	Round-nose pliers

1 Pour small amounts of the two parts of the two-part resin one by one into a mixing pot. Add a few drops of alcohol color and some glitter and stir into the resin well.

2 Use a toothpick to paint a thin layer of the colored resin evenly over the surface of the silver heart charm.

3 Carefully drop a flat-back crystal onto the heart, using tweezers.

4 Make up a jewel dangle (see page 27). Thread the jewel dangle and charm onto a jump ring.

5 Add the heart to the jump ring.

6 Thread the jump ring onto the chain. Attach a clasp to the chain with the remaining two jump rings.

lime candy bracelet

These vibrant flat beads may look just like candy, but the silver links set between them turn them into a stylish piece of jewelry. Here the elements are linked by threading the wire and then twisting it around the link directly, but you could use jump rings instead. For matching earrings, see page 59.

For matching earrings, see page 59.

estimated time to complete

Less than an hour

materials

Length of decorative chain with at least four large round links

24-gauge (0.5mm) silver wire

5 flat round lime magnesite 17mm beads

Lobster clasp

2 jump rings

tools

Wire cutters

Round-nose pliers

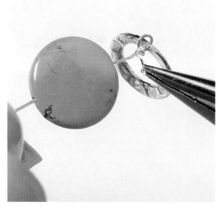

1 Carefully take apart the chain by opening up the individual jump rings between the decorative links.

2 Cut a 2½in. (6.5cm) length of wire and thread on a bead, then create a half loop at one end. Place one chain link on the half loop. Wind the wire around to secure the link to the bead.

3 Trim off any excess wire. Repeat to link all of the components together. Create a loop at the end of the last link. Attach a lobster clasp with a jump ring.

tip
Purchasing a chain with large decorative links and taking it apart to use the links in other ways is an inexpensive way to get interesting elements to use when making your own jewelry.

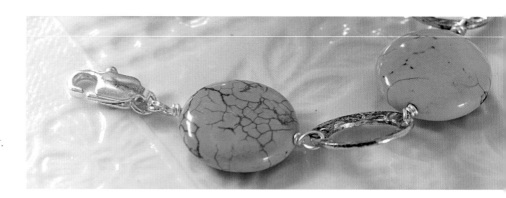

lime candy earrings

Bring on some sixties chic with these stylish earrings in bright candy colors! The trick with this design is to choose a decorative link for the bottom that is large enough in diameter for the bead to swing freely within it. For the coordinating candy bracelet, see page 56.

For the coordinating candy bracelet, see page 56.

estimated time to complete

Less than an hour

materials

2 large round links around 1in. (2.5cm) in diameter from a decorative chain

2 disks around 12mm in diameter from a decorative chain

2 jump rings

2 head pins

2 flat round lime 17mm beads

Pair of earring wires

tools

Round-nose pliers

1 Carefully take apart the chain by opening up the individual jump rings between the decorative links.

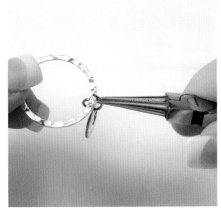

2 Open a jump ring and add one of the round links, then thread on the disk through the hole at one edge. Close the jump ring.

3 Thread a lime bead onto a head pin and create a loop with round-nose pliers. Use the loop to hang the bead from the jump ring used in step 2. The bead should dangle inside the round link.

4 Add the earring wire to the top of the disk. Repeat steps 1–3 to make the second earring.

lime candy earrings 59

spirals keychain

Friendly Plastic® is a wonderful material that can be colored and cut. Once it is heated, it becomes soft and pliable—so you can shape it or cut it into motifs using ordinary cookie cutters. It can be used to make all kinds of focal pieces for jewelry—see the Peyote Bangle on page 139 for additional ideas.

estimated time to complete

Less than an hour

materials

Friendly Plastic® silver/black strip

Oil-based heat-set paint or acrylic metallic paint in a color of your choice

Silicone-based glue

Keychain finding with circular disk

Swarovski™ crystal jewel finding

3 jump rings

Silver heart charm

tools

Scissors

Stylus or toothpick

Heat-resistant baking sheet

Heat gun

Small round cookie cutter

Bowl of cold water

Pliers

1 Cut a piece of Friendly Plastic® and place it on the heat-resistant baking sheet. Add a thin coating of oil-based paint over the surface with the tip of your finger, as described on page 32. Draw your chosen design into the paint, using a point such as a stylus or toothpick.

2 Heat the plastic gently with a heat gun for a few seconds until the plastic becomes soft and flexible. Do not allow the plastic to bubble, as it will get too hot and become sticky. Cut out the disk shape with a cookie cutter. Place the plastic in cold water to make it hard again, then pop out the disk.

tips

For some more ways of working with Friendly Plastic®, see pages 32–33 in the Techniques section.

If the plastic begins to bubble, it is too hot.

If the disk begins to curl, apply heat until it flattens out, then allow to cool on its own.

3 Apply silicone glue to one side of the circular finding disk. Stick the Friendly Plastic® disk onto the circular finding.

4 Use the point of the stylus to make a hole through the plastic to match the hole in the finding. Add the disk to the jewel finding and attach this to the main part of the keychain. Add the heart charm with a jump ring.

turquoise rain

This delicate necklace is made from flat rings of turquoise, which dangle freely from thin leather cord. The rich brown earthy tones of the leather bring out the golden tones in the turquoise beautifully, while the silver wire and spacers add a little sparkle to lighten the design.

estimated time to complete

About an hour

materials

24-gauge (0.5mm) silver wire

2 small flat turquoise rings

4 flat silver 4mm spacers

4 round green 4mm beads

1 large flat turquoise ring

2in. (5cm) length of silver chain

5 jump rings

Two 18in. (45cm) lengths of leather cord

Leather cord ends

tools

Wire cutters

Flat-nose pliers

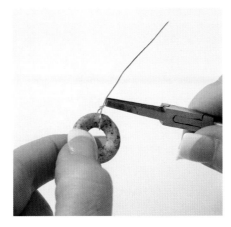

1 Cut a 3in. (7.5cm) length of wire. Loop wire through the hole in a small turquoise ring and back up, wrapping the end around the base of the wire to secure.

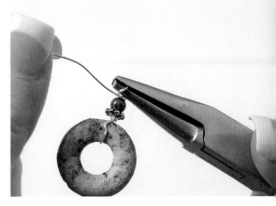

2 Thread a silver spacer and a round bead onto the wire. Create a loop with pliers and wind the end around to secure. Trim off any excess wire. Repeat with the other turquoise ring of same size. Wrap wire around both sides of the large turquoise ring, adding a spacer and round bead as before, creating a loop at the top and the bottom.

3 Attach the smaller rings to each end of the chain with jump rings. Attach the large turquoise ring to the chain, slightly off center. Thread both leather cords through the ring on the other side of the large turquoise ring.

4 Thread the cords into the cord end spiral. Press the base of the spiral firmly with pliers to secure. Repeat at the other end. Make an "S"-clasp and hook as described on page 29 and add to the cord ends with jump rings.

basic black bracelet

This pretty bracelet couldn't be simpler to make—and using elasticized cord means that it will fit a variety of wrist sizes. Do not pull the elastic cord too tightly around the wrist when measuring, because the thickness of the beads will take up some of the length and you don't want the bracelet to be uncomfortably tight.

estimated time to complete

Less than an hour

materials

Black elastic cord

9 faceted round black 8mm beads

9 faceted round black 5mm beads

18 silver bead caps

tools

Scissors

Beading board

1 Measure a length of black elastic cord by wrapping it around your wrist, then add on an extra 1in. (2.5cm) and cut to length.

2 Lay the beads out in the correct order on the beading board, with a bead cap on each side of the large bead and a small black bead between each set.

3 String the beads onto the cord, beginning with a silver bead cap, an 8mm bead, another bead cap then a 5mm bead. Repeat until all the beads are threaded on, finishing off with a 5mm bead.

4 Tie the elastic cord into a square (reef) knot, against the side of the beads. Trim the ends of the elastic down to about ¼in. (5mm) and tuck the ends out of sight inside the first large bead.

tip
For a wrist around 6½in. (16.5cm) in diameter, you will need 9 large and 9 small beads. Adjust the number of beads for a larger or smaller wrist, so when you have finished threading there is approximately ½in. (1cm) of elastic left free at each end.

basic black drop earrings

These earrings are based on intricate chandelier findings, so I kept the rest of the design very light, delicate and simple. The freely swinging chain at the base is very easy to add, but it creates a real sense of movement to the design, as well as making the earrings a little longer without adding any further weight.

estimated time to complete

Less than an hour

materials

6 head pins

2 faceted 6mm black Swarovski™ beads

4 faceted 3mm black Swarovski™ beads

2 chandelier findings

2 pieces of fine chain, each approx 2in. (5cm) in length

2 small jump rings

Pair of earring wires

tools

Round-nose pliers

Wire cutters

1 Thread one of the 6mm beads onto a head pin and bend the end around to form a loop.

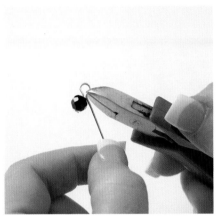

2 Snip off the excess wire with wire cutters.

3 Open the loop slightly and thread it onto one of the rings at the bottom of a chandelier finding. Close up again to form a neat ring. Repeat steps 1–3 to add a 3mm bead on each side.

4 Use a jump ring to add the end of a piece of chain to one of the bottom rings on one side of the chandelier finding. Loop the chain around and attach it to the other side of the finding with the second jump ring.

5 Attach the earring wire to the top of the chandelier finding, by opening the end ring as described on page 28. Repeat steps 1–5 to make the second earring.

sparkling bee

The design of this necklace was inspired by the purchased silver bee pendant, with its tiny black jewels that are echoed in the black beads. The design is kept simple, since the bee is so dramatic.

tip
If insects are not to your taste, any dramatic purchased pendant would work well with this design. Or make your own focal pendant using one of the ideas in the following chapter.

estimated time to complete

About an hour

materials

Bead stringing wire

2 crimp beads

3 jump rings

32 silver round 3mm beads

20 black faceted 4mm Swarovski™ crystal beads

9 silver 25mm curved tube beads

Bee-shape hanging focal bead

Lobster clasp

tools

Beading board

Wire cutters

Crimp pliers

Round-nose pliers

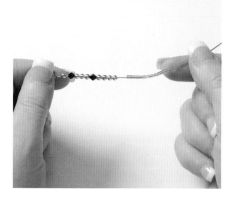

1 Lay the beads out on the beading board in the correct order. Attach bead stringing wire to a jump ring as described on page 24. Slide the first few beads over both strands of wire, then continue on just the main strand leaving the short end protruding from one side.

2 Continue threading the beads in the following sequence: silver, black, 3 silver, black, 4 silver, tube, black, silver, black, silver, black, tube, black, silver, black, tube, silver, black, silver, tube, silver, black, silver, black, silver. Add a tube, then repeat the previous sequence in reverse.

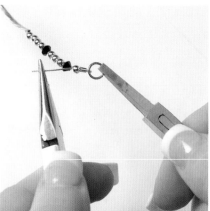

3 Add a crimp bead and jump ring to one end of the wire. Fold the end of the wire over the jump ring and back through the crimp bead and first silver bead.

4 Holding the jump ring with pliers, pull on the end of the wire to tighten the crimp bead up close to the jump ring. Crimp the bead to secure. Repeat steps 3–4 at the other end.

5 Find the center tube of the necklace. Using a jump ring, add the sparkling bee pendant so that it hangs in the center. Add the lobster clasp to the end jump rings.

under the sea

Mother-of-pearl comes from the inside of shells and I wanted a really watery feel to these earrings. The hammered finish on the square link is reminiscent of light rippling across water and the disks below hang freely as if they were waving gently in the current. For longer earrings, use a longer chain and add more disks.

estimated time to complete

Less than an hour

materials

2 silver pinch bails

2 square silver links

Pair of earring wires

2 large jump rings

2 short lengths of silver chain

10 mother-of-pearl 15mm disks

10 small jump rings

tools

Flat-nose pliers

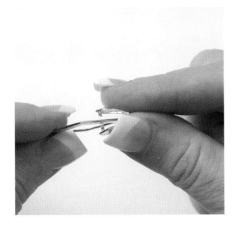

1 Locate the bail over the silver link. Press the sides of the bail together around the link.

2 Attach an earring wire to the top of the bail, then add a large jump ring to the end of a short length of chain and attach it to the bottom of the square link.

3 Use small jump rings to add five disks to the chain so that they hang decoratively at different lengths. Repeat steps 1–3 to make the second earring.

tip
These mother-of-pearl disks come in slightly different shades and may include bobbles or streaks—these are all part of a natural material and should not be considered as faults.

pagoda pendant

The jade-effect beads used in this pendant and the hanging piece made me think of Chinese pagodas with their hanging decorations—hence the name of this project. I combined the jade with dark polished wood, since many Chinese buildings are built in this material.

estimated time to complete

1–2 hours

materials

20-gauge (0.8mm) gold-color wire

Rectangular wooden link

2 flattened unakite beads

16 flat wooden disks

7 head pins

14 round wood beads

7 octagon yellow turquoise beads

6 unakite 4mm beads

12 antique-finish jump rings

10in. (25cm) of antique chain

Small square gold bead

tools

Wire cutters

Round-nose pliers

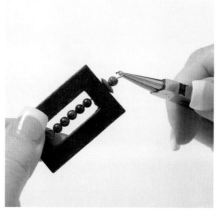

1 Cut a length of wire 1½in. (4cm) longer than the rectangular wooden link. Make a ring at one end and thread on a flattened unakite bead and a wooden disk bead. Thread the wire through the central hole at one end of the wooden link. Thread on six unakite beads before taking the end of the wire through the hole at the other end of the link.

2 Add another wooden disk and flattened unakite bead at the other end of the wire. Use pliers to create a loop, then cut off any excess wire. Add one of the flat wooden disks to the end ring with one of the jump rings.

3 Make a bead link as described on page 28 using a head pin, working in this sequence: round bead, wooden disk, octagon bead, wooden disk, round bead. Create a loop at the end. Make six more bead links the same. Join three of the bead links together with jump rings. Repeat with another three. Make a dangle with the last octagon bead as shown on page 27.

4 Join the two bead link sections with a 2in. (5cm) length of chain. Add another 4in. (10cm) length of chain to each free end with a jump ring. Attach the beaded dangle to the center of the necklace with a jump ring. Hang the wooden focal to the end of the dangle. Attach a jump ring to the end of each chain. Make the hook clasp by threading a short piece of wire through a small gold metal bead. Create a ring at one end and a hook at the other. Attach to the necklace with a jump ring and add an openwork finding for it to hook into on the other side.

tip

Openwork findings can be used to make great decorative clasps. To make this one even more attractive, I glued a small flat bead into the center.

handbag charm

These little dangle charms are not only popular as handbag decorations—they can be made into key rings instead, or used as elements on a necklace, or made up into earrings. In the same way, many of the other elements shown in this book could also be adapted to make charms; the possibilities are endless!

estimated time to complete

Less than an hour

materials

1 silver pinch bail

1 Swarovski™ leaf crystal pendant (topaz)

1 black faceted oval smoky quartz 8mm bead

1 silver bead cap

1 head pin

Short length of silver chain

Silver butterfly charm

1 large jump ring

Large silver lobster clasp

tools

Round-nose pliers

Wire cutters

1 Slightly open the bail with pliers and press the pins into either side of the crystal. Gently pinch the sides of the bail together to secure.

2 Thread a black quartz bead and bead cap onto a head pin. Bend the end of the pin with round-nose pliers to form a loop. Thread the loop onto a short length of chain. Close the loop and trim off any excess wire from the head pin.

3 Attach the charm chain and leaf crystal to the large lobster clasp with a jump ring.

heartfelt phone charm

Dangling charms on cell phones are particularly popular, especially with young ones. You easily personalize your phone if several of your friends have a similar model. Most cells have a built-in ring to take a hanging strap, and this is ideal to attach a charm to; the special loop top you need is widely available, so have fun creating your own dangles!

estimated time to complete

Less than an hour

materials

3 assorted silver heart charms

Short length of silver chain

4 silver jump rings

Loop top finding

tools

Round-nose pliers

Wire cutters

1 Add one heart charm to each end of the chain with jump rings.

2 Attach another heart charm about ¼in. (5mm) of the way down from the end of the chain with a jump ring.

3 Use the last jump ring to attach this ensemble to the loop top finding.

out of africa

Although these earrings use an animal-print pattern, the final result is definitely more sophisticated than tribal! The beads used are softly polished wood, contrasting with the patterned rectangles of silver that catch the light as they swing to add some sparkle and glitter to the design.

estimated time to complete

Less than an hour

materials

4 head pins

4 round 3mm silver spacer beads

4 silver bead caps

4 square 8mm wood beads

4 flat 4mm silver spacer beads

2 pieces of chain approx 1½in. (4cm) long

2 jump rings

Pair of silver disk earring wires

2 silver animal-print rectangles

tools

Round-nose pliers

Wire cutters

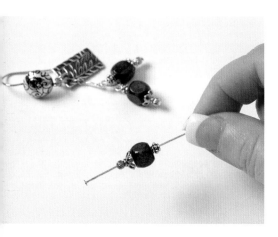

1 Thread a round spacer bead, bead cap, wood bead, and a flat spacer bead onto one of the head pins. Create a loop at the top with round-nose pliers. Cut off excess wire if necessary. Create three more bead dangles.

2 Attach one bead dangle to the end of one length of chain with a jump ring. Add another bead dangle just above the bottom with a jump ring.

3 Attach the chain to an earring wire with a jump ring.

4 Thread the silver rectangle onto the jump ring, and close it as described on page 28. Repeat steps 1–4 to make the second earring.

flower ring

Although this is one of the simplest projects in the book, it is designed to coordinate with the Peyote Floral bracelet on page 142, so when you have mastered the peyote beading technique you can make yourself a matching bracelet. The ring finding used here is adjustable, so one size fits all.

estimated time to complete

Less than an hour

materials

Silver ring blank

Silicone-based adhesive

2 crystal 4mm beads

2 pearl 4mm beads

1 large Lucite flower

1 green crystal leaf

1 Swarovski™ crystal bead

Glitter

1 Place a daub of silicone-based glue on the top of the ring. Place the pearl and crystal beads in the center.

2 Add the Lucite flower on the other side, allowing a portion of it to cover and sit against the beads at a slight angle to add extra interest.

3 Add the crystal leaf to one side. Glue a Swarovski™ crystal bead into the center of the Lucite flower. Add a little glitter to the center of the flower around the crystal bead, and on any exposed adhesive.

tip

Create a design that is asymmetrical and off-center. Overlapping elements make for a much more exciting and interesting design.

fabulous focals

The projects in this chapter are based around a central focal hanging pendant—sometimes a purchased finding and sometimes a handmade piece. The style of the necklace is often set by this focal pendant, so if you mix things around you can achieve quite a different look very easily!

dragonfly dreams

The dragonfly perched on the stone at the base of this necklace adds a real arty feel, but if you prefer something a little simpler you can omit it completely. When making a double strand like this, either keep both strands exactly the same or make one much simpler than the other to balance the design.

estimated time to complete

1–2 hours

materials

Bead stringing wire

15 fancy jasper 4mm beads

50 round faceted 4mm lemon stones

37 flat gold spacer beads

13 smoky quartz 5 x 9mm beads

Length of antique-finish chain

Double-strand copper toggle fastener

2 jump rings

4 bicone 4cm lemon stones

2 antique crimp beads

Octagonal focal pendant of choice

26-gauge (0.4mm) wire

Antique brass dragonfly

Silicone-based glue

tools

Round-nose pliers

Wire cutters

1 Thread beads onto a length of the bead stringing wire to make up a dangle with loops at each end, as described on page 27. Work in the following order: jasper bead, faceted lemon stone, gold spacer, smoky quartz crystal, gold spacer, faceted lemon stone and finally another jasper bead. Make up seven of these and join them with 2in. (5cm) lengths of antique-finish chain between each. Attach the ends to one ring of the double-strand fastener.

2 Add a jump ring to the beading wire as described on page 24. Make up the beaded strand in the following order: gold spacer, 3 faceted lemon stones, gold spacer, smoky quartz crystal, gold spacer, 3 faceted lemon stones, gold spacer, bicone lemon stone. Repeat once. The center sequence is gold spacer, 3 faceted lemon stones, gold spacer, smoky quartz crystal, gold spacer, 6 faceted lemon stones, gold spacer, smoky quartz crystal, gold spacer, 3 faceted lemon stones, gold spacer. Repeat the first sequence twice. Attach the end jump ring as described on page 24. Use the jump rings to add the beaded strand to the double strand fastener.

3 Add the octagonal focal pendant by wrapping a 6in. (15cm) length of wire around one side and through the hole twice. Thread on a gold spacer, and a jasper bead. Make a loop over the center of the beaded strand, then twist the end around to secure. The antique brass dragonfly can be added permanently with a small dab of silicone-based glue.

victorian charm necklace

The antique-finish findings and delicate filigree give a vintage feel to this design, which is essentially very simple to make. The charms used here are quite large, but smaller ones would work just as well, as long as the larger chain is also reduced to a suitable scale. Feel free to substitute charms to your taste or desired theme.

tip

This necklace uses ready-made crystal dangles—but if you can't find suitable ones, make your own from crystal beads using the technique described on page 27.

estimated time to complete

1–2 hours

materials

Large antique flower focal pendant

4 large antique finish jump rings

20in. (50cm) length of antique-finish large-link chain

Antique-finish clasp of choice

2 large heart charms

2 key charms

2 small heart charms

4 faceted amethyst 8mm crystal dangles

8 amethyst crystal bead dangles

9 small antique-finish jump rings

9½in. (24cm) length of antique-finish fine chain

1 amethyst crystal heart

tools

Round-nose pliers

1 The large flower focal pendant has two rings on the reverse to support its weight. Use two large jump rings to join it to the center of the large-link chain, spacing them so that the flower hangs straight. Add the two parts of the clasp to the ends of the chain using the other two large jump rings.

2 Plan out the order on the necklace, placing the larger charms nearer the center flower and working outward. Add the charms to the chain with the smaller jump rings. Add the four faceted crystal dangles by opening up the ring on the top, threading it onto the chain, and then closing the ring again.

3 Attach the crystal heart to the center of the fine chain with a small jump ring. Space out the eight small crystals evenly on each side and attach them to the chain with their top rings. Join the end of the fine chain to a link of the large chain about 2½in. (6.5cm) from one end with a small jump ring; repeat on the other side.

silver leaf necklace

This dramatic necklace is far easier to construct than it may look at first glance. Simply thread beads onto bead stringing wire for the top section; the beaded links are made individually and joined together. The silver leaf pendant on its own looked a bit too plain, so I added a few fun jewel dangles to liven it up.

estimated time to complete

1–2 hours

materials

Bead stringing wire

4 crimp beads

4 jump rings

Toggle fastener

2 faceted black crystal 12mm beads

34 silver seed beads

24-gauge (0.5mm) silver wire

2 filigree links

28 faceted black crystal 6mm beads

2 large clear crystal links

2 large smoky crystal links

Medium silver circle link

Purchased cluster of bead dangles (or make your own of choice)

Large silver leaf pendant

tools

Round-nose pliers

Flat-nose pliers

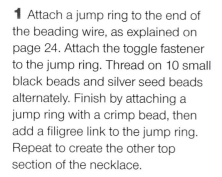

1 Attach a jump ring to the end of the beading wire, as explained on page 24. Attach the toggle fastener to the jump ring. Thread on 10 small black beads and silver seed beads alternately. Finish by attaching a jump ring with a crimp bead, then add a filigree link to the jump ring. Repeat to create the other top section of the necklace.

2 Cut a 2in. (5cm) length of wire and thread on a small black bead, silver seed bead, large black bead, silver seed bead and another small black bead. Create a loop at each end. Cut off any excess wire. Repeat once and then create four smaller beaded links in the same way using seed bead, small black bead, seed bead.

3 Join the beaded sections together in the following order; beaded top section made in step 1, clear crystal link, small beaded link, smoky crystal link, then another small beaded link. Repeat for the other side, using the photograph on page 89 as a guide.

4 Open out the top ring on the purchased beaded cluster, as described on page 28, and use it to attach the cluster to a medium size silver circle link.

5 Open the large jump ring at the top of the silver leaf pendant and add the silver circle link complete with the beaded cluster. Close the jump ring again carefully.

6 Open the loop at the end of one of the final small bead links on the necklace and thread it onto the hole in the silver circle link. Repeat on the other side.

silver leaf earrings

These earrings were designed to coordinate with the Silver Leaf Necklace on page 88—they use the same faceted black beads and a smaller version of the crystal link. The dangling beads echo the dangling jewels at the base of the necklace, but the earrings are much lighter in weight, making them comfortable to wear.

estimated time to complete

Less than an hour

materials

2 faceted black 12mm crystal beads

4 head pins

4 silver seed beads

Short lengths of silver chain

2 faceted black crystal 6mm beads

2 small crystal bead links

Pair of earring wires

tools

Round-nose pliers

1 Thread one of the large beads onto a head pin, add a silver seed bead, and create a loop at the top. Attach a 1in. (2.5cm) length of chain to the loop.

2 Repeat step 1 with one of the small beads and a slightly shorter length of chain. Add both chains to the bottom of the crystal link.

3 Add an earring wire to the ring at the top of the crystal link. Repeat steps 1–3 to create the second earring.

indian summer earrings

Reminiscent of traditional Indian jewelry, these earrings use natural semi-precious stones in the rusts and gold colors predominant in early Fall. Semi-precious stones are a natural material, so they come in a varying colors and shades; check through the available stones if you want something specific. For a coordinating pendant, see page 94.

estimated time to complete

Less than an hour

materials

24-gauge (0.5mm) silver non-tarnish wire

4 round silver 3mm spacers

4 round unakite 4mm beads

4 flat silver 5mm spacers

4 square orange 6mm beads

10 square flat 6mm shells

4 small round brown wooden 5mm beads

Pair of earring wires

tools

Wire cutters

Flat-nose pliers

Round-nose pliers

1 Cut a 2½in. (6.5cm) length of silver wire. Thread the beads onto the wire in the following order: round spacer, unakite bead, flat spacer, one square bead. Add five of square shells and then repeat with the other beads in reverse order.

2 Cross the right-hand wire over the top of the left-hand wire, approximately ¼in. (6mm) above the beads.

3 Twist the left-hand wire closely a few times. Cut the excess end of the right-hand wire off neatly, leaving the left-hand wire straight.

4 Using the round-nose pliers, create a round loop at the end of the wire, then twist the end around the base and cut off any excess.

5 Open out the ring at the end of the earring wire as described on page 28, and thread the wire loop onto it. Close the ring with pliers. Repeat steps 1–5 to make the second earring.

indian summer pendant

The silver wire combined with a selection of natural semi-precious stones gives a real ethnic feel to these earrings. Here the stones are in rich shades of brown and rust, but they would look just as stunning in other colors such as turquoise or reds. The matching earrings are shown on page 92.

estimated time to complete

Less than an hour

materials

3 head pins

6 round unakite 4mm beads

3 flat silver 5mm spacers

6 square flat 6mm shells

1 square orange 6mm bead

1in. (2.5cm) length silver chain

5 medium-size jump rings

1 flat pearl 15mm disk

1 large silver jump ring

Length of leather cord

24-gauge (0.5mm) silver wire

2 small silver jump rings

Toggle fastener

tools

Flat-nose pliers

Round-nose pliers

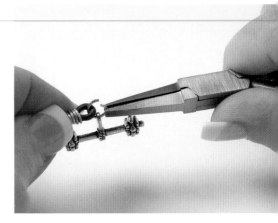

1 Make up three beaded dangles on head pins as described on page 27, using the beads, spacer, and flat square shells as desired. Add a medium jump ring to each end of the chain and add the pearl disk to one end to make the fourth dangle. Open up the large jump ring and thread on the four dangles.

2 Thread the remaining three medium jump rings onto the leather cord. Thread the large jump ring through all three medium jump rings and close with pliers.

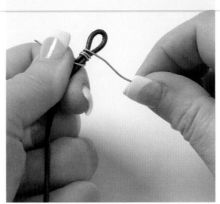

3 Fold the end of the cord over to form a loop. Wrap a short length of wire tightly around the cord to hold the loop in place. Repeat at the other end.

4 Attach the toggle fastener to the loop with small jump rings.

buttons 'n' bows

This necklace is very random and freeform—
I wanted to create the look of found treasures, using
vintage buttons, odd leftover beads, sparkly bits,
and lengths of chain. It reminded me of going
through Grandma's jewelry box on a rainy day…
filled with hidden treasures.

tip
The base of the necklace is made
from buttons piled together and
just glued in place, with other
decorative bits added afterward.

estimated time to complete
1 hour, not including drying time

materials
Selection of new and vintage buttons

Silicone-based glue

Selection of odd beads, crystals, and bead caps

3 lucite flowers

Antique-finish wire

Odd lengths of antique-finish chain

Brown crystal seed beads for the fastener

1 decorative bead for the fastener

1 small silver spacer bead for the fastener

24-gauge (0.5mm) copper wire

1 large bead for the fastener

1 glass bead for the fastener

Selection of silver spacers

Selection of odd beads and crystals

Antique-finish jump rings

tools
Wire cutters

Round-nose pliers

Toothpick

1 Arrange and layer buttons in a
crescent shape. Use dabs of
silicone-based glue to fix into place.

2 To create a little sparkle, stick on a
selection of beads, crystals, bead
caps, and lucite flowers. Allow the
glue to dry.

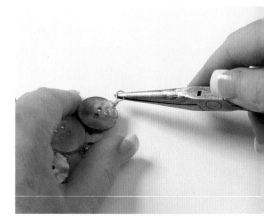

3 Loop a piece of antique-finish wire
around a pair of round-nose pliers
and twist the ends together. Trim the
wire ends to ½in. (1cm). Repeat for
the other side. Glue the loops onto
the reverse side of the pendant on
each side.

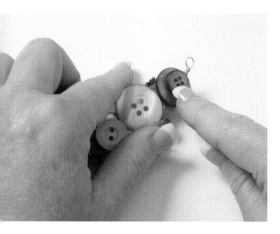  

4 Place a button over the wire ends to hide them and give a finished look, and glue in place. Repeat on the other side.

5 Place a dab of glue on the center back of the crescent in two places, approximately 1in. (2.5cm) apart. Press the ends of a short length of antique-finish chain into the glue with a wooden toothpick.

6 Place a button over the ends of the glued chain to hide them and finish off, then allow to dry. Place an arrangement of beads on a head pin and attach to the chain to make a dangle.

7 To make the loop of the clasp, cut a short length of wire and thread on approximately 30 brown seed beads. Curve the wire around into a loop.

8 Twist the two ends of the wire together to secure them. Check to make sure that the loop will fit over the bead that will be used to form the other side of the clasp.

9 Thread a decorative bead and a small silver spacer bead onto the double thickness of wire. Create a loop at the end and trim off any excess wire.

10 Cut a piece of copper wire 3in. (7.5cm) long. Thread the large bead onto the center of the wire, then take both ends of the wire and twist them together. Add a glass bead onto the double thickness of wire. Attach to a 6–8in. (15–20cm) piece of chain with a jump ring.

12 Make up a series of beaded dangles using odd beads, crystals, spacers, and bead caps. Assemble the necklace using jump rings, placing the different bead units randomly and spacing them with short lengths of chain.

11 Create a loop with the round-nose pliers and wrap the end of the wire around the base of the loop. Trim off any excess wire. Attach this "hook" to a separate piece of 6–8in. (15–20cm) chain with a jump ring.

arabian nights pendant

There is no need to make every element in a project from scratch—in this design, a handmade pendant is added to a purchased necklace. Combining purchased and handmade elements is a great way to make the most of your available time.

estimated time to complete

1 hour

materials

20in. (50cm) silk beading thread/cord

Rectangular 40mm wood link

3 round brown 6mm beads

2 flat 20mm beads

4 bronze bead caps

8 flat 6mm beads

1 long black-and-white 25mm bead

1 long wood 12mm bead

13 bronze seed beads

1 triangular brown bead

1 head pin

1 green 3mm bead

1 diamond-shape filigree finding

1 purchased necklace

tools

Scissors

Round-nose pliers

Wire cutters

1 Cut two lengths of cord, each approximately 10in. (25cm) in length. Fold the cord in half and place the loop through the center of the wooden link. Thread the ends of the cord through the loop and pull. Repeat for the second strand. Knot all the cords together to secure.

2 Thread a round 6mm bead and the flat 20mm beads onto all the cords, then knot again below the beads to hold them in place.

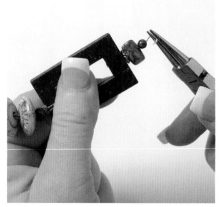

3 Divide the four strands out and thread a random selection of the remaining beads onto each strand individually. Knot the ends to secure.

4 Thread a head pin through the hole at the top of the link. Add a spacer bead, brown bead, and green round bead. Create a loop with the round-nose pliers, and cut off the excess wire.

5 Choose a filigree finding that is larger than the width of the wooden link and bend the sides of it so it wraps around the wood link and grips firmly.

tips

If you want to make your own necklace section, you could create something similar with braided (plaited) and knotted thread.

When using cord or thread, beads with larger holes are easier to work with.

6 Use the ring at the top of the link to hang the pendant from a purchased necklace—or you can make a necklace of your own based on one of the other projects in the book.

very cherry earrings

These round, bright red beads reminded me of sun-ripened cherries on the tree, so I created these dangling earrings with their swinging fruitlike beads. The earring wires used here have a chain incorporated, but alternatively you could add a length of chain to a plain earring wire to get the same effect.

estimated time to complete

About an hour

materials

18 round red 4mm beads

18 head pins

Pair of silver earring wires with chains

tools

Round-nose pliers

Wire cutters

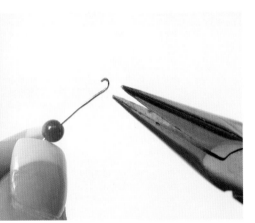

1 Thread one of the beads onto a head pin.

2 Shorten the head pin as required, so that the beads will hand at different lengths. Bend the end of the head pin into a loop, using the round-nose pliers.

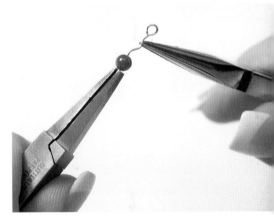

3 To add interest, leave the wire a little bit longer and bend it into a decorative shape.

4 Attach the beads at different heights of the earring chain, using the ring at the end of the head pin.

hearts and pearls bracelet

Pearls have always been popular to wear at weddings, and what could be more romantic than pearls combined with silver hearts? This charming bracelet is really easy to construct, and would look stunning with many different outfits. For matching earrings, see the design on page 106.

estimated time to complete

1 hour

materials

5 natural pearl 8mm beads

6 silver heart-shape 10mm links

24-gauge (0.5mm) silver wire

2 jump rings

Lobster clasp

tools

Wire cutters

Round-nose pliers

1 Pull a length of wire off the reel, but don't cut it off yet. Thread a pearl bead and a heart link onto the wire.

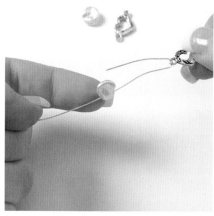

2 Bend the free end of the wire back on itself by about 1in. (2.5cm) to form a loop.

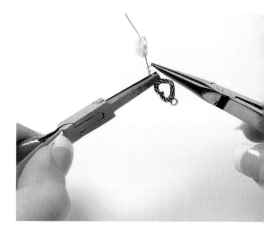

3 Twist the end of the wire around several times to hold the heart link in place.

4 Add a second heart link on the other side of the pearl bead, bend the wire over as in step 2 then cut the wire off the reel, leaving an end of around 1in. (2.5cm). Continue in this way until you have the required length of bracelet—check that it fits your wrist. Add the clasp using jump rings as described on page 28.

pearl drops

You don't have to use ready-made findings—the hooks on these earrings have been handmade by bending silver wire into shape. To add extra interest, the wire is twisted randomly and decoratively around the outside of the pearl as well as being threaded through it. For a matching bracelet, see the design on page 104.

For a matching bracelet, see the design on page 104.

estimated time to complete

Less than an hour

materials

24-gauge (0.5mm) silver wire

2 natural pearl 8mm beads

2 silver heart-shape 10mm links

tools

Wire cutters

Round-nose pliers

Metal file

1 Working off the spool, add a pearl bead onto the wire. Create a loop at the top with the round-nose pliers and wind the wire around to secure.

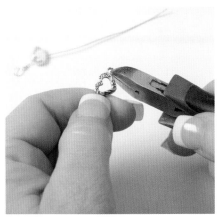

2 Snip off the rings on either side of the heart-shape link.

3 Cut approx 4in. (10cm) length from the wire and bend it in half near the pearl threaded on in step 1. Place the heart on the wire.

4 Thread the wire through the heart link and then twist it around itself to hold the heart link firmly in place. Wrap the remaining wire decoratively around the bead.

tip

After you cut the loops off the sides of the heart, you may have some sharp edges. Just file these down gently until the sides are smooth again.

To make the earring hook, just bend a length of wire into shape with a ring at one end, using the photograph opposite as a guide.

chinese jade

The warm tones of copper combine so well with jade that these earrings are always a winner. As an alternative to heat-setting ink, you could etch the design onto the copper using a copper etching kit. To get a matching pair of earrings, reverse the shape before cutting out the second piece.

estimated time to complete

About an hour

materials

Piece of copper sheet

2 copper jump rings

24-gauge (0.5mm) silver wire

4 flat wooden spacer disks

2 octagonal yellow, turquoise, or jade 18mm beads

2 round brown 6mm beads

2 earring wires

tools

Heat-setting inkpad for metal in black

Design stamp

Heat gun

Metal shears

Metal file

Needle tool

Round-nose pliers

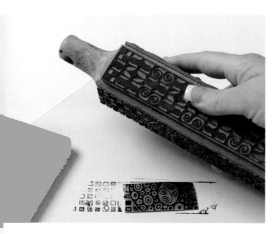

1 Using an inkpad and stamp, print a suitable design onto a small piece of copper.

2 Heat the copper with a heat gun to set the ink design. Cut out two matching shapes from the copper, using metal shears.

3 Carefully file away any sharp edges with a fine metal file.

4 Use a needle tool to punch a hole near the top of each metal shape.

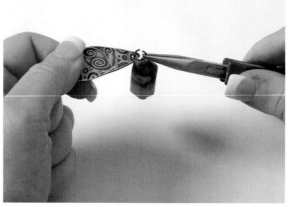

5 Thread a spacer disk, octagonal bead, spacer disk, and brown bead onto a 2½in. (6.5cm) length of silver wire and make a loop at each end, as described on page 28. Add the copper shape to one end with a copper jump ring and the earring wire to the other end. Repeat steps 1–5 to make the second earring.

multi-strand designs

While these designs may look complex, they merely combine several strands together for a slightly bolder look. These designs can incorporate several identical strands or a combination of beaded strands and chains. Really, the sky is the limit with these designs—and remember you can always substitute your favorite beads for those shown to achieve a very personalized look.

orange blossom bracelet

The orange blossom design on the clasp inspired the name of this project, and having decided on this, it seemed obvious to choose beads in orange and pink to keep to the theme. The heavy cluster of crystal dangles around the toggle is reminiscent of ripe hanging fruit.

estimated time to complete

1–2 hours

materials

Silver-colored bead stringing wire

4 crimp beads

6 jump rings

2 faceted pink crystal 6mm beads

4 faceted clear crystal 10mm beads

4 faceted peach crystal 8mm beads

1 packet of orange seed beads

10 silver bead caps

1 packet of assorted orange and pink glass bead mix

6 head pins

Toggle fastener with orange flower

tools

Crimp pliers

Round-nose pliers

Wire cutters

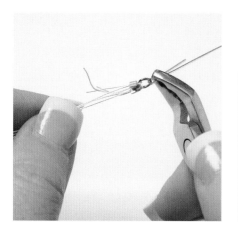

1 Measure your wrist, add 1½in. (4cm), then cut four strands of bead stringing wire to this length. Thread two wires through a crimp bead, over a jump ring, and back through the crimp bead. Crimp the bead with pliers to secure. Repeat for the remaining two strands.

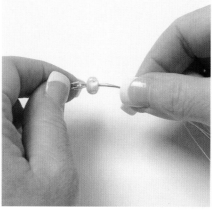

2 Thread a bead onto all the wires and slide it down to the end to conceal the crimp beads.

3 Start threading on assorted crystal beads. Each large bead goes onto one wire, but at intervals a orange seed bead is threaded onto two threads together. This gives the larger bead a floating effect.

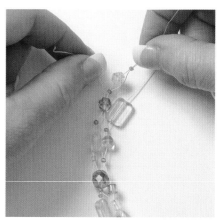

4 Thread a orange seed bead onto a different pair of wires each time, to achieve a woven look to the design.

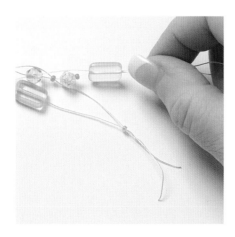  

5 Carry on in this way to the end, using the larger beads in a random order but scattering the seed beads regularly over the pattern.

6 At the far end, slide the threads into a crimp end as in step 1, then use jump rings to add the fastener.

7 Make up a series of crystal dangles, as described on page 27.

8 Add clusters of crystal dangles at each end near the fastener.

mountain mist pendant

The soft blues and greens in this pendant are reminiscent of the misty woods in the Ozark Mountains where I live, hence the name of this project. The plain strand of turquoise crystal beads is the base of the design and sets the overall tone.

1 Mix and pour the two-part resin, as described on page 31, to make the hanging pendant.

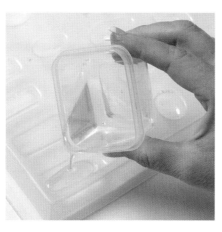

2 Pour the resin into the mold, filling to just below the top edge.

3 Scatter glitter flakes over the surface of the resin and set aside to set for at least 12 hours. Push the pendant out and clean up, as described on page 31.

estimated time to complete

1–2 hours excluding resin curing time

materials

Two-part resin	Bead stringing wire
Glitter flakes	Silicone base adhesive
Sticker	2 bead caps

Alcohol ink in color of choice

1 pale blue 8mm crystal bead (for pendant)

63 turquoise 6mm crystal beads (strand 1)

64 clear 2mm seed beads (strand 1)

Pack of bead mix in turquoise and blues (strands 2 and 3)

94 clear 2mm seed beads (strand 2)

4 silver bead caps (strand 2)

2 round silver 4mm spacer beads (strand 2)

4 flat silver 4mm spacer beads (strand 2)

10 crimp beads (strand 3)

56 clear 2mm seed beads (strand 3)

3 jump rings

Lobster clasp

tools

Mixing bowl	Fine sandpaper
Pendant mold	Hand drill
Toothpick	Wire cutters
Scissors	Round-nose pliers

tip

When pouring resin, it is always worth pouring a few extra pieces to use for future projects.

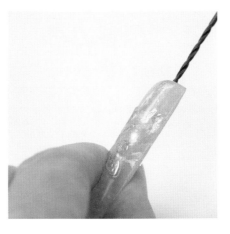

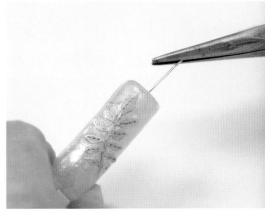

4 Choose a suitable sticker to fit the size of the pendant. Color over the surface of the sticker with a little alcohol ink. Place the sticker on the front of the pendant and rub it down gently.

5 Using a small hand drill, make a small hole in the center at the top end of the pendant.

6 Cut a short section of wire and dip the end into a little adhesive. Push the end into the hole in the pendant.

7 Thread a bead cap, a crystal bead, another bead cap, and finally a seed bead onto the wire.

8 Use the round-nose pliers to bend the wire to form a loop at the center top of the pendant. Cut off any excess wire.

9 Make up two strands of the necklace with beads threaded on wire. Make up the final strand with floating beads at intervals using crimp beads, as described on page 24. Use jump rings to add the pendant to one of the strands of the necklace, and the clasp to the ends.

raindrops necklace

The thin silver beading wire gives this delicate necklace an ethereal look—crimp beads are used to make the beads stay in position along the wire as if they were floating in thin air. The faceted beads reflect the light, and the square link also has glitter included in the acrylic, so it sparkles, too.

estimated time to complete

1 hour for necklace and earrings

materials

Silver-colored bead stringing wire

10 crimp beads

4 jump rings

2 flat rectangular blue 12mm glass beads

6 round faceted blue 6mm glass beads

1 silver bead cap

2 large jump rings

1 blue acrylic 12mm square link

1 head pin

1 lobster clasp

tools

Crimp pliers

Wire cutters

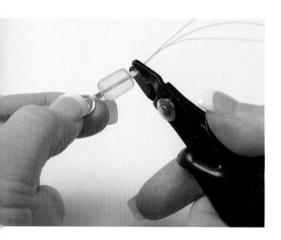

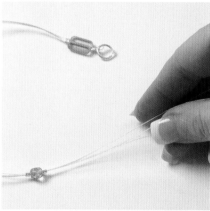

1 Cut three 20in. (50cm) strands of beading wire. Use a crimp bead as described on page 24 to add a jump ring to the end, and then add a rectangular blue bead and secure it in position with another crimp bead.

2 Thread a crimp bead, round blue faceted bead, and a second crimp bead on all three strands. Do not crimp them in place yet.

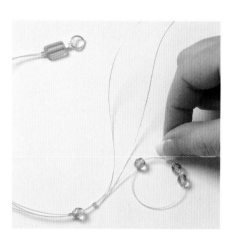

3 Take just one strand of wire and thread three faceted beads onto it. Thread the end back through the first of the three beads to create a loop.

tip

To make the matching earrings, make up two more square links with dangles, as shown in step 5. Then simply add an earring wire to the top of each square link using jump rings.

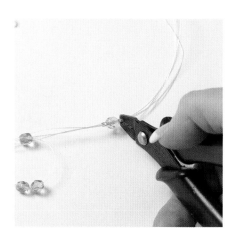

4 Thread a crimp, flat blue glass bead, crimp, and jump ring onto the end and finish as described in the first step. Trim off the excess bead stringing wire. Add a crimp bead, blue faceted bead, and a second crimp bead on all three strands. Do not crimp. Arrange the beads and wire evenly in position, and then compress all the crimp beads with the pliers to hold everything in place.

5 Open a large jump ring and add it to the square link. Make up a dangle bead using a blue bead, head pin, and bead cap as described on page 27. Add the dangle bead to the jump ring and close the ring.

6 Use another large jump ring to add the square link to the loop at the base of the necklace. Attach the lobster clasp to the necklace ends.

art nouveau necklace

Incorporating ribbon into jewelry designs can instantly give a vintage feeling. Here, a metallic antique-look ribbon is threaded through a handmade chain to soften its lines and make it look much more curvaceous and art nouveau. The ribbon also adds a rich bronze tone, which is reflected in the color of the crystals.

estimated time to complete

1–2 hours

materials

22-gauge (0.6mm) gold-color wire

26 faceted round bronze 8mm crystal beads

Approx 24in. (60cm) narrow metallic antique-look ribbon

1 oval filigree finding

Piece of wooden dowel

3 jump rings

1 antique-look oval pendant finding

1 head pin

1 faceted clear 4mm bead

1 gold bead cap

tools

Wire cutters

Round-nose pliers

Scissors

1 Cut a 1½in. (4cm) piece of wire and thread on a crystal 8mm bead. Use the round-nose pliers to make a loop.

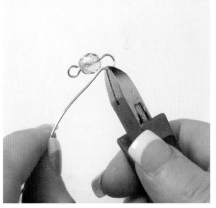

2 Create another loop on opposite side of the bead. Trim off the excess wire on both sides.

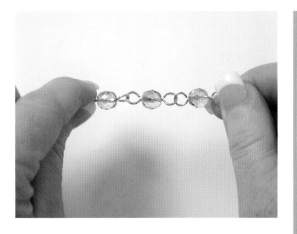

3 Repeat steps 1 and 2 for the remaining 8mm crystal beads. Join the loops together to create the chain.

tip
Findings are often more readily available in plain silver or gold, but if you want an antique finish—
or want gold for a particular project when you only have silver, or vice versa—you can easily change the color with a little Rub 'N' Buff®. See page 29 for the technique.

4 Thread the antique ribbon in and out through the links of the chain on either side of each bead, working right around the necklace. Knot the ribbon onto the first and last link to secure it in place.

5 Pull the ribbon mesh apart to give a more decorative and lacy appearance. Press the filigree finding around a wooden dowel to shape it into a bail.

6 Thread the rounded filigree finding onto the necklace and add a jump ring through both sides of the base to hold the oval pendant.

7 Create a crystal dangle as described on page 27 and add it to the inside of the oval pendant. Make an S-clasp and hook as described on page 29 and attach it to the necklace with jump rings.

sands by the sea

A sandy beach may look as if it's one color at first glance, but when you get up close there are lots of different colors shades and tones—just as in this lovely necklace. To make it, I simply threaded the chips at random onto the beading wire and then braided the strands together loosely.

estimated time to complete

1–2 hours

materials

Bead stringing wire

6 crimp beads

6 jump rings

Multi-strand clasp

3 strands of citrine chips each approximately 20in. (50cm) long

Simulated glass stone beads in coffee quartz (optional)

tools

Crimp pliers

1 Cut three strands of bead stringing wire 19in. (47.5cm) in length and attach each to a jump ring with a crimp bead, as described on page 24. Attach each jump ring to a ring on one side of the multi-strand clasp. Start threading the crystal chips onto the wire.

2 Keep on threading the wire with the chips in a random order until all three strands are covered, adding the glass beads at random if desired. Braid (plait) the three strands loosely together. Finish each with a jump ring and crimp bead, as before.

3 Attach the jump rings on the ends of the strands to the corresponding rings on the other side of the clasp.

tip

The clasp of this necklace also serves as a focal piece, which allows versatility when wearing this design. It can be worn as an elegant strand of beads with the clasp in the back, or the clasp can be worn in the front—or even to one side as another fashion option.

coral cascade

estimated time to complete

1–2 hours

materials

Monofilament beading material (Supplemax)

Packet of assorted 10/0 seed beads in neutral colors

2 crimp ends

Pendant of choice

Large silver link

Large jump ring

Lobster clasp

tools

Curved beading needle for bead spinner

Bead spinner

Crimp pliers

Seed-bead necklaces look fantastic—don't be put off by the idea of stringing thousands of tiny beads, because using the bead spinner makes it really fast and easy! On this necklace I have left the strands in straight lines, but they can also look very effective twisted together or braided as on page 124.

1 Make a knot in the end of a length of monofilament to stop the beads sliding off the end as you thread.

2 Slide the other end of the beading thread into the slot in the beading needle and pull it down firmly into place.

tip

Add a dab of glue to the crimp before placing the ends of the beading thread into it. This will prevent the thread slipping out before you have a chance to crimp it in place.

3 Hold the curved end of the beading needle down into the seed beads. Spin the bowl so the needle begins to pick up a random assortment of beads.

4 Bead up several strands for the necklace. Take the ends of the strands together and place them in the crimp part of a crimp end. Fold over the sides of the crimp with the crimp pliers.

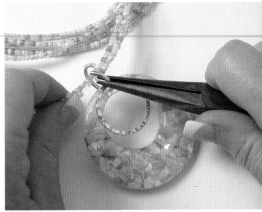

5 Add the pendant and the large silver link together to a few of the beaded strands, using a large jump ring. Add the clasp.

autumn leaves

estimated time to complete

1–2 hours

materials

Silver bead stringing wire

6 crimp beads

6 jump rings

Magnetic multi-strand clasp

1 packet of bead mix in bronze colors

4 silver spacer bars

tools

Scissors

Crimp pliers

Beading board (optional)

Golds and bronzes are Fall colors, so they seemed the ideal choice to use for this bracelet with its magnetic leaf clasp. With bead mix you can sort the beads so you can create repeating designs if you prefer, but I rather like the random effect you get just by picking up the first bead that comes to hand and threading it on.

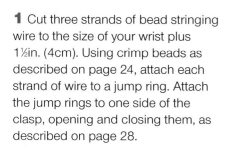

1 Cut three strands of bead stringing wire to the size of your wrist plus 1½in. (4cm). Using crimp beads as described on page 24, attach each strand of wire to a jump ring. Attach the jump rings to one side of the clasp, opening and closing them, as described on page 28.

2 Begin threading a random selection of beads onto each of the separate strands. If you prefer, work out your chosen design on the beading board before you begin.

3 After approximately 1½in. (4cm), thread each strand through its corresponding hole in one of the spacer bars.

tips

Designing this project on a beading board makes this project so much simpler, particularly if you don't want a random effect but to create more regular patterns.

Magnetic clasps are a great way to add a focal point to a bracelet or necklace that does not look like a fastening but can be used as part of the design instead.

4 Continue threading the beads, following the established design and adding spacer bars at 1½in. (4cm) intervals or as desired. Attach a jump ring to the end of each bead stringing wire with a crimp bead as shown on page 24. Attach this jump ring to the other end of the magnetic clasp.

waterfall lariat

You don't need to worry about length with lariat designs—just clip the end on anywhere, so the mother-of-pearl circles and watery agates just cascade down.

estimated time to complete

1 hour

materials

24-gauge (0.5mm) silver wire

10 large agate beads

9 mother-of-pearl disks

14 large jump rings

20in. (50cm) decorative silver chain

6 bead caps

6 head pins

Short lengths of fine chain

8 small jump rings

1 large decorative silver link

tools

Wire cutters

Round-nose pliers

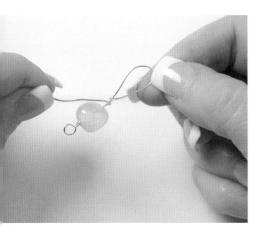

1 Cut a 1½in. (4cm) length of wire and thread it through one of the agate beads. Make a loop at one end, as described on page 27. Fold the wire at the other end in half to make a double thickness, and twist the end around to secure it.

2 Use the pliers to pinch the wires together and shape the double section over into a neat hook. Bend the tip out slightly to finish it off, as shown on page 30.

3 Make three of the agate beads up with a wire loop on each side, as described on page 28. Join four of the mother-of-pearl disks alternately to the agate beads to form a chain, using two large jump rings between each. Add the agate bead with the hook to one end of this chain, and one end of the decorative silver chain to the other.

4 Combine the remaining agate beads with bead caps on head pins to make agate dangles. Cut four pieces of fine chain to various different lengths and add an agate dangle to one end of each. Attach a mother-of-pearl disk slightly above with a jump ring. Using small jump rings, hang the chains randomly at intervals along the last 7in. (17.5cm) of the decorative chain.

5 Attach an agate dangle on a large jump ring to the silver circle pendant, and hang on the decorative chain 8in. (20cm) from the end, near the first hanging chain. Add the final agate dangle and mother-of-pearl disk to the end of the decorative chain with a jump ring.

earth day

Rich earthy colors are combined here in a braided multi-strand bracelet, with silver spacers used to add a little sparkle. If the idea of both threading and braiding at the same time seems too daunting, make sure that the links you choose for the third strand are small enough to slip through the larger links.

estimated time to complete

1–2 hours

materials

Bead stringing wire

6 crimp beads

10 jump rings

72 unakite 4mm beads

16 flat spacer beads

4 round beige 8mm beads

3 large beige links

2 short lengths of chain

2 small round green links

2 medium round green links

1 toggle fastener

tools

Scissors

Wire cutters

Crimp pliers

1 Measure your wrist and add 1½in. (4cm). Cut the stringing wire to length. Attach a jump ring to the end of the stringing wire with a crimp bead, as described on page 24. Thread on unakite beads, then finish off with another crimp bead and jump ring, as detailed on page 24.

2 Make up a second strand in the same way, beginning with 4 unakite beads, flat spacer, 8mm bead, flat spacer, large link bead. Repeat this sequence twice more, then finish with a flat spacer, 8mm bead, flat spacer, 4 unakite beads. Attach a jump ring to each end with a crimp bead.

3 The third strand is made in the same way with unakite beads and small and medium green links, but must be woven in and out of the larger link beads as you work, because the green links will not thread through the large link beads. Finally, weave the first strand through the link beads.

4 Join all three stands onto the end of a short length of chain using a jump ring. Repeat at the other end. Add the two halves of the fastener to the ends of the chain.

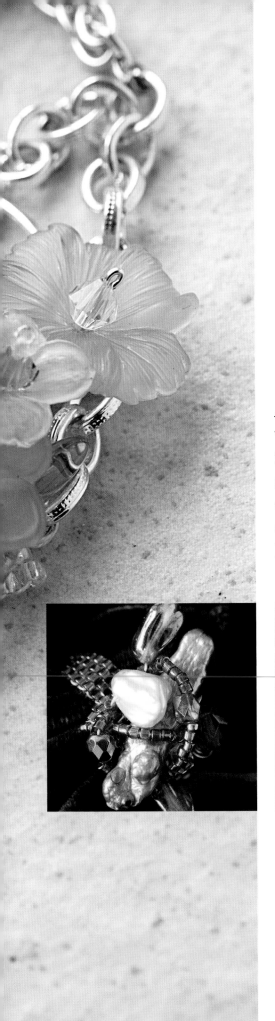

bead weaving and wire wrapping

As you become more skilled at jewelry making, you will want to make pieces that rely less on purchased findings. Many of the projects in this chapter use silver wire coiled around by hand to hold the stones and create movement in the design—and in some of these projects we use the technique of peyote bead weaving.

moonlight flower necklace

I find the idea that there are flowers that only bloom at night fascinating, and they were the inspiration for this necklace with its midnight colors. Despite their dark shades, the beads used have a blue/green iridescence that makes them glow like beetle's wings in the light of the moon.

estimated time to complete

1–2 hours

materials

14 black iridescent long beads

Bead stringing wire

1 faceted crystal bead

Packet of 10/0 dark blue seed beads

2 crimp beads

6 jump rings

Black polyester cord chain

3 dark blue teardrop beads

Toggle fastener

tools

Scissors

Wire cutters

Crimp pliers

Round-nose pliers

1 Thread 14 iridescent beads onto a 10in. (25cm) length of beading wire. Take the end of the wire and thread it back through all the beads.

2 Pull the wire tight to pull the beads into a flower. Add a crystal bead to one strand of the wire.

3 Pull the beaded wire down to the direct opposite side, so that the crystal bead sits in the center of the flower. Wrap the end of the wire between the petals once to secure the bead in place.

4 Pull the wire tight and thread the end back through the bead to the other side. You will now have two wires on the same side. Thread the un-beaded wire through the center bead and out the opposite side.

5 Thread a crimp bead and several seed beads onto the wire. Loop the wire back through the first two beads, then the crimp bead. Pull tight and crimp. Repeat the same steps on the opposite side, making a smaller loop.

6 Crimp the other loop in place, then cut off any excess wire.

7 Use a jump ring to attach the flower to the center link in a cord chain. Make up three dangles with the teardrop beads, as described on page 27.

8 Use jump rings to add a bead dangle to the bottom loop of the flower, and one to the chain on each side. Add the toggle fastener to each end of the chain.

peyote bangle

The peyote stitch technique is a way of making beaded sections that can be used in all kinds of ways. Here I have made a strip that is then wrapped around a length of heavy wire to make a beaded bangle—much easier than trying to bead in the round. Since the beading is stepped like a brick wall, the edges interconnect beautifully.

estimated time to complete

3–4 hours

materials

Friendly Plastic® silver/black strip

Selection of different designs and colors of Friendly Plastic® strip

Filigree finding

Silicone-based glue

Monofilament beading thread

Red cube 3mm beads

20-gauge (0.8mm) wire

2 silver bead caps

2 large silver beads

2 silver jump rings

tools

Scissors

Round-nose pliers

Heat-resistant baking sheet

Heat gun

Oval cookie cutter

Stylus or toothpick

Collapsible-eye beading needle

Wire cutters

1 Create a Friendly Plastic® oval, as described on pages 32–33. Choose a filigree finding bigger than the oval shape. Place it on the back of the oval, using pliers to wrap the sides around to the front to hold the finding in place.

2 Glue a focal piece onto the front of the pendant with silicone-based glue.

3 Using red cube beads, make up a length of peyote beading 20 beads long by 7 rows high, as described on page 36.

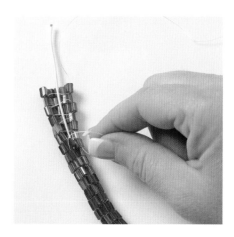

4 Weave the end of the thread from the last row through the second bead of the first row, then back through the third bead of the last row, fourth bead of the first row and so on backward and forward along the length.

5 Thread a 12in. (30cm) length of wire through the weaving on the back of the bracelet.

6 Begin pulling up on the thread from the beginning to curve the beading around over the wire, so the wire is then threaded through a beading tube.

7 Thread the wire through a bead cap. Add a silver bead and finish with a loop. Trim off the excess wire if necessary. Repeat for the other side.

8 Gently curve the wire around to form the bangle.

9 Use two jump rings to add the oval you made in steps 1–2 to the two ends of the beaded section.

tips

The bangle does not open up, so make sure it is big enough to fit over your hand. Measure around your closed fist to estimate the size. Alternatively, you could use a hook at one side of the oval instead of a jump ring.

As a substitute for Friendly Plastic®, substitute a favorite pendant or brooch and give it an updated look.

You can also follow the instructions for working with resin on page 31. Add a light coat of resin over the top of the Friendly Plastic® to create a glasslike, shiny appearance. Allow at least 24 hours to cure.

peyote floral bracelet

This project also uses the peyote stitch technique to create a beaded section as a base to attach the flowers. The silver chain is doubled to give the bracelet a little more weight. For a matching ring, see the Flower Ring on page 80.

1 Make a beaded square 12 beads wide by 12 rows high in white seed beads, using the peyote stitch technique detailed on page 36. Add the chain with jump rings to the sides.

2 Bring the thread up through the beaded section from the back through the center front of the square. String on a seed bead, Lucite flower, crystal, and seed bead.

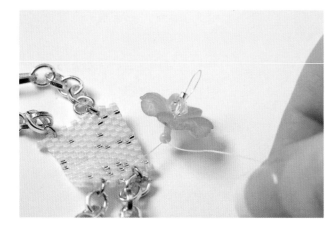

3 Thread the needle back through the crystal, flower, seed bead, and through the square to the bottom. Pull tight. Continue stringing on a variety of flowers. Be creative with the floral centers by using a combination of crystals and seed beads. Finish by stringing on accent beads and leaves.

estimated time to complete

3–4 hours

materials

Wildfire® beading thread

Silver/White 10/0 seed bead mix

Green 10/0 seed beads

2 lengths silver chain each 6in. (15cm)

4 jump rings

5 large Lucite flowers

9 Swarovski™ crystal beads

3 Lucite trumpet flowers

4 tiny Lucite flowers

7 green glass dagger beads (leaves)

7 small turquoise crystal beads

1 lilac crystal bead

tools

Scissors

Collapsible-eye beading needle

Round-nose pliers

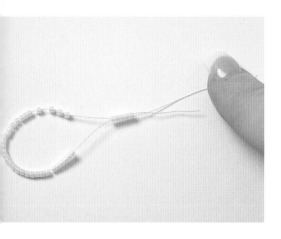

4 Tie a 4in. (10cm) length of Wildfire® thread to one end of the chain and thread on approximately 28 white seed beads. Take the end of the loop back through the first four beads to create a beaded loop for the clasp. Add a few floral beads to the end and knot. For the toggle on the other side, tie the thread to the end of the chain. String on green seed beads, Lucite flower, crystal, and a seed bead. Thread the needle over the seed bead and back through all remaining beads, then knot to secure. The flower fits into the loop like a toggle.

tip
The flowers are placed in a random pattern, so each bracelet will turn out differently depending on the types of flower shapes that are used.

5 Tie the beaded loop to the end link of the chain, with a tiny flower and crystal added to hide the join. Add a short beaded section at the other end, ending in a Lucite flower.

crystal cluster ring

Random clusters of beads and crystals can be very attractive in their own right, and here they are added to a ring made of peyote beading, which is made using delica seed beads. Although the final ring looks quite dramatic and chunky, it is still very easy and light to wear.

estimated time to complete

3–4 hours

materials

Wildfire® beading thread

Packet of iridescent delica seed beads

Long pearl bead

2 green crystals on head pins

3 small faceted crystal beads

1 amethyst faceted crystal

1 pearl bead

tools

Collapsible-eye beading needle

1 Using the peyote stitch technique detailed on page 36, make a square 8 beads wide by 8 rows high with beading thread and delica beads. Make up a rectangle in the same way, 22 beads wide and 4 rows high. Join the two pieces together by weaving between alternate beads at the edges, using the beading thread.

2 Gently pull the thread tight so that the two pieces interconnect without a visible joint.

3 Bring the thread up to the front and through the long pearl bead, and then down and out through the back to secure the bead to the front of the ring.

4 Bring the needle back up to the front, thread on some seed beads, take over the pearl bead, then take the needle down to the back again to secure.

5 Continue "sewing" beads onto the ring to create the desired pattern. To finish the ring, connect the other side of the band as in steps 1–2 and secure with a square knot.

tip

You will need seed beads for the peyote stitch section of the ring, but the decoration on top can be quite random, so you can use up odd beads.

This ring will fit an average size finger. To make it bigger or smaller, make the peyote stitch sections longer or shorter.

heart to heart bracelet

estimated time to complete

1–2 hours

materials

6 faceted round crystal 10mm beads

24-gauge (0.5mm) non-tarnish silver wire

10 small jump rings

Approx 9in. (23cm) pearl mesh ribbon

2 large jump rings

5 Swarovski™ crystal 10mm heart dangles

tools

Wire cutters

Round-nose pliers

Scissors

With this design I set out to create a light and feminine bracelet using Swarovski™ crystal hearts and silver metallic ribbon. Joining the crystal beads with simple links would have introduced an unwanted feeling of regular repeats, so instead I used wire to join them, wrapping it around the beads in curving swoops and spirals.

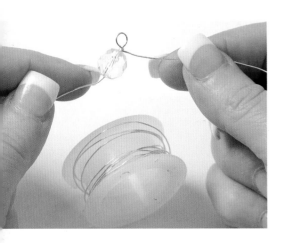

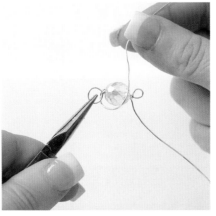

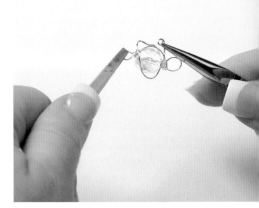

1 Take one of the large round crystal beads and thread it onto a 4in. (10cm) length of the wire. Bend the wire into a loop on both sides of the bead, leaving long ends.

2 Start twisting one of the wire ends across the bead randomly to create a decorative pattern of wire around one side of the bead.

3 Repeat on the other side with the other end. Curve the ends into flat spirals and twist them to sit against the side of the bead.

tip

If you want to make a longer necklace but don't have enough beads or ribbon, just add some short lengths of chain to each end before adding the clasp.

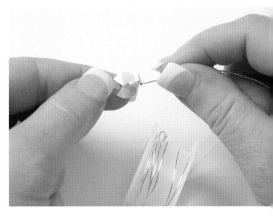

4 Make several more wire-twisted crystal beads in the same way. Join the beads together using five small jump rings. Attach a large jump ring to each end.

5 Thread the ribbon through the jump rings, zigzagging it through opposite sides of the bracelet. Knot the ends to the jump rings at each end of the bracelet.

6 Working off the spool, thread wire through a heart crystal leaving approximately ½in. (1cm) extending. Wind this extension around the wire to secure.

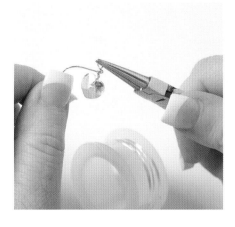

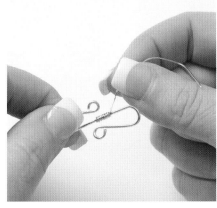

7 Create a loop at the top with round-nose pliers. Wrap the wire around to secure and trim off any excess wire. Repeat steps 6–7 with the other hearts. Attach the hearts to the bracelet with jump rings.

8 Make an S-shape clasp, as described on page 29. Wrap a short length of wire around the central section to add decorative embellishment to it.

9 Attach the two sections of the clasp to the opposite ends of the bracelet, fixing onto the jump rings.

fairy flower pendant

You could almost imagine a fairy constructing this light and delicate necklace from cobwebs and dewdrops. The gauzy ribbon is pretty, but you could use a fine chain or a seed bead strand. For earrings, add an earring wire instead of ribbon in step 4.

estimated time to complete

About an hour

materials

24-gauge (0.5mm) silver wire

22-gauge (0.6mm) silver wire

1 round faceted crystal 10mm bead

1 pink crystal seed bead

1 white mother-of-pearl flower

16in. (40cm) length of organza ribbon

2 crimp ends

1 lobster clasp

2 jump rings

tools

Round-nose pliers

Crimp pliers

Scissors

tip

This technique of wire wrapping is very freeform. There are no specific measurements; simply create as many or as few loops and squiggles as you like.

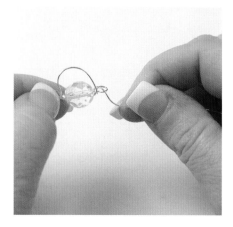

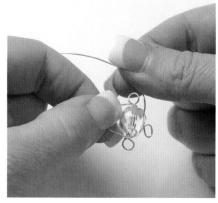

1 Cut an 8in. (20cm) length of 24-gauge (0.5mm) wire; make a loop at one end. Thread on the crystal bead. Create a loop at the other side. Bend the end of the wire over and wrap around the loop on the opposite side. Repeat on the other side.

2 Continue looping and winding the wire as desired. Trim off the excess wire when the required effect has been achieved.

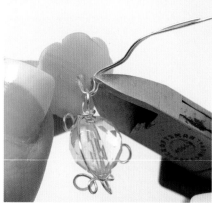

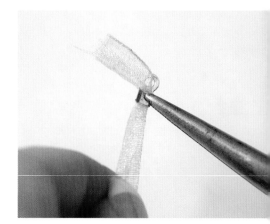

3 Thread a pink crystal seed bead onto the center of a 2in. (5cm) length of wire. Pinch together and thread on the mother-of-pearl flower.

4 Form a loop in the doubled wire with round-nose pliers and thread on the crystal bead. Bend the loop down to secure and trim any excess wire close to the back of the flower. Thread onto the ribbon.

5 Place one end of the ribbon in a crimp end and fold the crimp over with pliers to secure. Trim off any excess ribbon with scissors. Repeat on the other side. Attach the lobster clasp with jump rings.

nature watch

A watch does not have to be on a plain strap—this one is an exciting piece of jewelry. The watch face is just a standard type, with wire threaded through the lugs instead of the normal pins. Choose beads to coordinate with a favorite outfit—or make several in different colors.

estimated time to complete

1–2 hours

materials

18-gauge (1mm) silver wire	Watch face
24-gauge (0.5mm) silver wire	Bead mix in bronze colors
	8 silver spacers

tools

Wire cutters	Metal file
Round-nose pliers	

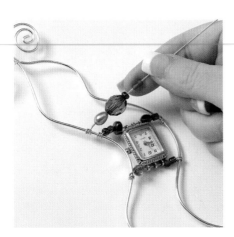

1 Cut a piece of 18-gauge (1mm) silver wire at least 15in. (38cm) long. Use the round-nose pliers to bend the ends into curving spirals, then shape the wire into a series of curves. Repeat with a second length of wire.

2 Place the two lengths of wire so the end spirals point in opposite directions and touch at the base. Wrap a short length of 24-gauge (0.5mm) wire over the two main wires to join them securely together. Repeat at the opposite end.

3 Cut a 4in. (10cm) length of 24-gauge (0.5mm) wire. Wrap around an outside wire in the center. Thread on a bead, take the wire through the watch face lugs, then add another bead. Wrap the other end of the wire around the other side wire. Repeat on the other side of the watch face.

4 Add a random selection of beads and silver spacer beads on cross wires spaced at irregular intervals along the two parallel main wires. Secure the ends of the wire by wrapping around main side wires.

5 Make sure that there are no sharp ends of wire protruding anywhere—file any sharp edges smooth if necessary. Gently bend the side wires into a curve to form a bracelet that fits your wrist.

tip

Wire is available in a variety of widths and colors. Colored wire will give a more whimsical look, and you could also use multi-colored beads for a fun and jazzy effect.

leather beaded bracelet

Leather cords combined with beads in simple but effective bracelets have been popular for years, but this variation incorporates twists and spirals in silver wire to add a little more interest to the basic design. The variation with the large bead has a large decorative clasp, but the smaller one has a more discreet fastener.

estimated time to complete

Less than an hour

materials

Large oval ceramic bead

24-gauge (0.5mm) non-tarnish silver wire

Thick leather cord

2 small beads

2 jump rings

Decorative clasp for leather cord

tools

Wire cutters

Flat-nose pliers

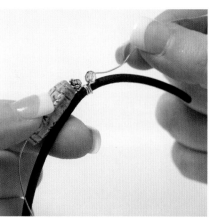

1 Thread the large bead onto a 4in. (10cm) length of wire. Lay the bead on the leather cord and wrap the wire around it on one side to hold it firmly in place.

2 Add a small bead to the wire and twist the wire around the cord again to hold this in place.

3 Curve the end of the wire into a decorative spiral. Repeat steps 1–3 on the other side of the large bead.

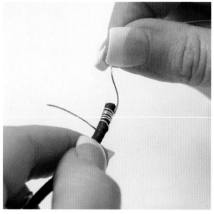

4 Cut a 1in. (2.5mm) length of the wire and wrap it tightly around one end of the leather cord.

tips

When you are wrapping the wire, don't cut it off the spool at the start—just pull out a length to work with and only cut it off when you come to attach the end. That way you are not limited as to the amount of wire that you have to work with.

You can adjust the length of the clasp by coiling the spiral of the hook a little more.

  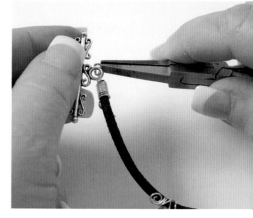

5 Form a loop at the end of cord with round-nose pliers. Cut off any excess wire, leaving ½in. (1cm) remaining.

6 Twist the end of the wire into a decorative spiral. Repeat steps 5–6 at the other end of the leather cord.

7 Add a decorative clasp to one end of the leather cord with a jump ring, opening it as described on page 28. If the main bead is smaller, choose a smaller clasp that is more in scale, as shown in the variation (see page 157).

mossy oak necklace

There is a camouflage fabric called mossy oak that is in exactly the same greens and browns as the oval beads used in this necklace. The leather cording seemed the ideal material to hang them on, but I brightened up the design with a few shell disks, silver spacer beads, and bead caps.

estimated time to complete

About an hour

materials

90in. (225cm) length of leather cord

12 head pins

5 flat oval turquoise 25mm beads

4 round brown 12mm beads

2 round 15mm shell disks

3 oval 20mm shell disks

22 unakite 4mm beads

9 flat silver spacer beads

2 large decorative silver spacer beads

2 medium decorative silver spacer beads

2 small decorative silver spacer beads

4 triangular orange 6mm beads

3 small wooden 4mm disks

11 flat 6mm shell disks

24-gauge (0.5mm) silver wire

8 jump rings

2 silver cone ends

Lobster clasp

tools

Scissors

Round-nose pliers

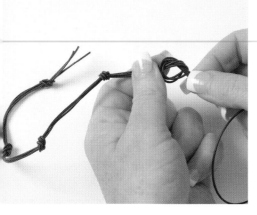

1 Cut three 30in. (75cm) lengths of leather cord. Knot them all together approximately 1in. (2.5cm) from the end. Continue creating a knot approximately every 1in. (2.5cm) down the length of the cord. Pull the knots tight.

2 Make up the jewel dangles from the head pins, beads, and disks, following the instructions on page 27. The center turquoise oval is the longest piece, with a silver spacer and 3 shell disks, and is hung from a wooden disk.

tips

If you start with the leather cords approximately 30in. (75cm) in length, the finished necklace will be around 18in. (45cm). For a longer necklace, cut the starting cords longer.

Try on your design and view it in a mirror as you go along, so you can make adjustments to the bead order to make sure that it hangs comfortably and naturally.

3 There are 19 dangles in total, all made up to different lengths. Four of them are longer, made with turquoise ovals, two on each side of the center. The others are also made in pairs, with one on each side of the center.

4 Attach the dangles to the cording by opening up the top loop or jump ring and closing it over the leather cord. Arrange the dangles on the cords so the shorter ones are to the outside and the longer ones to the center, creating a rough curving shape to the necklace.

5 Thread a 2in. (5cm) length of wire through the knot on the end of the leather cord and twist one end around to hold it in place, then cut off this end flush with the twist. Trim off the excess cord, leaving a length approximately ¼in. (5mm) remaining.

6 Thread a cone onto the wire and compress slightly with pliers to hold it in place over the knot. Use the round-nose pliers to bend the end of the wire protruding from the cone into a loop. Add a cone at the other end of the cords in the same way. Add the two halves of the clasp, one to each wire loop.

macramé necklace

As the saying goes, "What's old is new," and macramé is becoming popular once again in jewelry design. The decorative knots are easy to make and create a lovely open and lacy look. This necklace design includes crystal dangles as well, which were chosen to reflect the color of the macramé cord.

estimated time to complete

About an hour

materials

Macramé cord in a shade of choice

5 head pins

3 faceted 20mm beads of choice

2 faceted peach 6mm beads

8 silver bead caps

5 faceted green 4mm beads

1 square silver and crystal charm

5 small jump rings

2 large jump rings

1 toggle fastener

tools

Scissors

Adhesive tape

Round-nose pliers

1 Cut 6 cords 48in. (120cm) long. Knot all the cords together at one end. Lay them out with the knot at the top and the threads extending down toward you. Tape over the ends to hold the cords in place.

2 Take the right-hand cord over the central cords and under the left-hand cord, holding it in place on the right with your finger.

3 Take the left-hand cord under the central cords and thread it through the loop in the right-hand cord, holding it in place on the left with your finger.

4 Pull on the two cords evenly to tighten the knot you have just made up under the original knot. This completes half the square knot.

5 Take the left-hand cord over the central cords and under the right-hand cord, holding it in place on the left with your finger.

6 Take the right-hand cord under the central cords and thread it through the loop in the left-hand cord, holding it in place on the right with your finger.

7 Pull on the two cords evenly to tighten the knot you have just made gently up under the original knot. This completes one complete square knot. Repeat steps 2–7 six more times.

 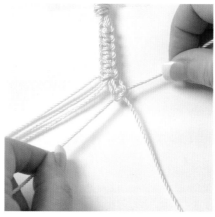

9 This completes one square knot on the right-hand side. Repeat steps 2–7 on the left-hand side to make a complete square knot on the left.

8 Divide the cords into two groups of three. Repeat steps 2–7, using only the three cords on the right.

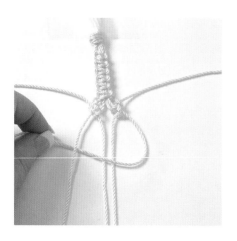 

10 Bring all the strands into the center again, then move strands 1 and 6 off to the side and repeat steps 2–7, using only the central strands 2, 3, 4, and 5.

11 This completes a square knot in the center. Repeat steps 8–9 to make a square knot on the right and on the left again.

12 Bring all the strands into the center again. Repeat steps 2–7 twice. This completes one section of the necklace. Repeat steps 8–12 six more times, then repeat steps 2–7 seven more times to finish the necklace.

13 Knot the ends and trim off the excess cord. Make up five jewel dangles with the head pins and crystals, as described on page 27, and attach to the center of the necklace with jump rings.

14 Open one of the jump rings and attach it to one end of the necklace. Attach one half of the toggle fastener.

15 Attach the other half of the toggle fastener to the other end of the necklace in the same way.

swarovski™ wire dangle earrings

Create a dramatic yet delicate effect using Swarovski™ crystals. Even though they are generally more expensive than glass beads, the fantastic sparkle they give means they are worth the extra money. These earrings appear minimalist, but they will look absolutely stunning when the light catches them.

estimated time to complete
Less than an hour

materials
22-gauge (0.6mm) silver wire
6 head pins
2 topaz faceted 6mm Swarovski™ crystals
2 gold bead caps
4 pink faceted 4mm Swarovski™ crystals
2 lime faceted 4mm Swarovski™ crystals

tools
Wire cutters
Round-nose pliers

1 Make the shape of an "S" loop from silver wire, as described on page 29. Thread the head pin through one of the topaz crystals and add the bead cap. Curve the end of the head pin round into a loop.

2 Hook the loop over the S-clasp, then close it fully. Make up the two pink crystals with the remaining head pins in the same way and add them to the rings in the middle of the loop, one on each side.

3 Thread the lime crystal onto the end of a 1½in. (4cm) length of wire and twist the end into a loop using the round-nose pliers.

4 Use the round-nose pliers to shape the other end of the wire into an earring hook. Repeat steps 1–4 to make the second earring.

gypsy-style necklace

Of all the jewelry that I make, this necklace always brings me the most compliments—people just seem to love it. Don't be put off by the complex-looking design—in fact, this is a really easy project to make because there are no rules: just do what seems to look right.

estimated time to complete

1–2 hours

materials

Metal disk

Decorative silver disk (optional)

Silicone-based glue

Silk beading cord in a neutral color

1 green bead

Jasper disk

Approximately 80–120 miscellaneous semi-precious and glass beads in random sizes, shapes, and colors

Miscellaneous metal spacers

Wooden disk

Head pins

2 short lengths of chain

2 jump rings

Toggle fastener

tools

Scissors

Collapsible-eye beading needles

Round-nose pliers

1 If desired, glue the decorative silver disk onto the metal disk with silicone-based glue. Unwrap the silk cord from the spool and cut two 36in. (90cm) lengths. Thread a beading needle onto the end of each cord.

2 Thread both cords through the back of the metal disk and tie a knot. Thread one cord over the green bead, through the center hole, and under the other side. Thread the other cord upward through the center hole and over the top of the bead. Tie a knot to secure this bead in place.

3 String a selection beads onto one cord, knotting every so often to give a decorative element to the design. Some beads are strung on one strand, some on both. Continue adding beads as desired to finish this side of the necklace.

4 To add a multilayered look, tie on a short section of additional cording and thread on more random beads. Tie the end onto a loop link.

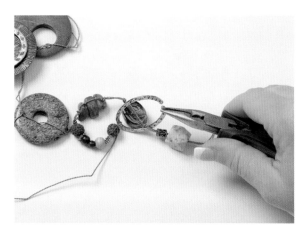

5 Add a loop link to the other beaded cord. Continue adding small sections of beaded cord to this side as desired, threading in and out of loops or beaded sections randomly.

6 Finish by knotting all the cords together at one end. Tie on the wooden disk.

7 Make up some dangle pieces using head pins, as described on page 27, and hang these from the cords toward the base of the necklace.

8 Open up the links at one end of a short section of chain and add a section of chain to each end of necklace. Attach the halves of the toggle fastener to the ends of the chain using the jump rings.

tips

This design is a great way to use all the leftover beads from previous projects. There is no wrong way to design: simply let it flow by stringing random beads onto thread and tying sections together.

For this design, work from the center point out toward the ends, so you can balance the shape of the design as you go.

Resources

Linda Peterson
www.lindapetersondesigns.com
www.lindapetersondesigns.blogspot.com
linda@lindapetersondesigns.com
+1 417 443 2072

US SUPPLIERS

Artbeads.com
11901 137th Ave. Ct. KPN
Gig Harbor, Washington 98329
+1 253 857 3433/+1 866 715 2323
www.artbeads.com
For Swarovski crystals.

Artistic Wire
440 Highlands Blvd
Coatesville
PA 19320
+1 610 466 0000/+1 866 423 2325
www.artisticwire.com
*For non-tarnish silver and copper wire.
Sells wholesale to retail companies, or
see online for stockists.*

Beadalon
www.beadalon.com
*For bead stringing materials,
miscellaneous findings, and bead
making tools. Sells wholesale to retail
companies, or see online for stockists.*

Blue Moon Beads
Creativity Inc.
7855 Hayvenhurst Avenue
Van Nuys, CA 91406
+1 800 727-2727/+1 818 988-8280
www.bluemoonbeads.com
Sells wholesale to retail companies.

CGM Inc.
19611 Ventura Boulevard
Suite 211
Tarzana, CA 91356
+1 800 426 5246
www.cgmfindings.com

Crafts, etc.
Online store
1-800-888-0321
www.craftsetc.com

Darice Inc
13000 Darice Parkway
Park 82
Strongsville, OH 44149
+1 866 432 7423
www.darice.com
*For the Jill MacKay Collection.
Sells wholesale to retail companies.*

EK Success
www.darice.com
*For Jolee's Jewels.
Sells wholesale to retail companies,
or see online for stockists.*

Fire Mountain Gems
1 Fire Mountain Way
Grants Pass, OR 97526-2373
+1 800 355 2137
www.firemountaingems.com

Halcraft USA
+1 914 840 0505
www.halcraft.com
*Sells wholesale to retail companies,
or see online for stockists.*

Hobby Lobby
Stores nationwide
www.hobbylobby.com

Jewelry Supply
Roseville
CA 95678
+1 916 780 9610
www.jewelrysupply.com

Jo-Ann Fabric and Craft Store
Stores nationwide
1-888-739-4120
www.joann.com

Land of Odds
718 Thompson Lane
Ste 123, Nashville, TN 37204
+1 615 292 0610
www.landofodds.com

Michaels
Stores nationwide
1-800-642-4235
www.michaels.com

Mode International Inc.
5111-4th Avenue
Brooklyn, NY 11220
+1 718 765 0124
www.modebeads.com

A.C. Moore
Stores nationwide
1-888-226-6673
www.acmoore.com

Plaid Enterprises
+1 800 842 4197
www.plaidonline.com
Jewelry and other craft supplies.

Rings & Things
P.O. Box 450
Spokane, WA 99210-0450
+1 800 366 2156
www.rings-things.com

Rio Grande
7500 Bluewater Road. NW
Albuquerque, NM 87121
+1 800 545 6566
www.riogrande.com

Shipwreck Beads
8560 Commerce Place Dr. NE
Lacey, WA 98516
+1 800 950 4232
www.shipwreckbeads.com

Stormcloud Trading Co.
725 Snelling Ave. N
St. Paul, MN 55104
+1 651 645 0343
www.beadstorm.com

Thunderbird Supply Company
1907 W. Historic Rte. 66
Gallup, NM 87301
+1 800 545 7968
www.thunderbirdsupply.com
www.americanbeads.com
Online sales only.

Unicorne Beads
404 Evelyn Place,
Suite D Placentia, CA 92870
www.unicornebeads.com

Wig Jig
P.O. Box 5124
Gaithersburg, MD 20882
www.wigjig.com

CANADIAN SUPPLIERS

Abra-kad-abra Collection
763 Mont-Royal East Metro
Mont-Royal
Montreal (QC) H21-1W8
www.abra-kad-abra.com

Bead and Craft
International Inc.
7357 Woodbine Avenue
Unit #1 Suite# 314
Markham (ON) L3R-6L3
+1 416 640 0168
www.beadandcraft.com

Bead Box Inc.
17-B Cartier Avenue
Pointe-Claire Village
Pointe-Claire (QC) H9A-1Y5
+1 514 697 4224
beadbox@bellnet.ca

The Beadery
446 Queen Street West
Toronto (ON) M5V-2A8
+1 416 703 4668
www.thebeadery.ca

BeadFX Inc.
128 Manville Road, #9
Scarborough (ON) M1L 4J5
+1 877 473 2323/+1 416 701 1373
www.beadfx.com

A Beautiful Gift
5460 Yonge Street, Suite 103
North York (ON) M2N-6K7
+1 416 226 5762
www.abeautifulgift.ca

Bedrock Supply
9435-63 Avenue
Edmonton (AB) T6E-0G2
+1 780-434-2040
www.bedrocksupply.ca

Canada Beading Supply
11A-190 Colonnade Road South
Ottawa (ON) K2E 7J5
+1 613-727-3886
www.canbead.com

UK SUPPLIERS

All About Crafts
www.allaboutcrafts.com
Supplies Friendly Plastic® and other crafting materials.

Burhouse Ltd
Quarmby Mills
Tanyard Road
Oakes
Huddersfield
West Yorkshire HD3 4YP
+44 (0)1484 485100
www.burhouse.com

Cookson Precious Metals
59-83 Vittoria Street
Birmingham, B1 3NZ
+44 (0)845 100 1122
+44 (0)121 200 2120
www.cooksongold.com

Craftime
Craftime Limited
Unit B2. 3 Willow Drive
Sherwood Business Park
Annesley
Notts NG15 0DP
Telephone: 01623 722828
www.craftime.com
For bead making tools, supplies, beads, and findings. Mail-order company.

Creative Beadcraft
1 Marshall Street
London W1F 9BA
+44 (0) 207 734 1982
www.creativebeadcraft.co.uk
Visit the London shop or buy online.

Jilly Beads Ltd
+44 (0)1524 412728
www.jillybeads.com
Buy online or by phone.

Wires.co.uk
18 Raven Road
South Woodford
London E18 1HW
+44 (0) 208 505 0002
www.wires.co.uk

Index

Acknowledgments

I would like to send out a very special thank you to several people who have made this book possible.

To Molly Duran of Touchstone Beads in Springfield, Missouri, who helped me brainstorm ideas. To my editorial team: Marie Clayton, Liz Dean, Cindy Richards, and Sally Powell—thank you for your hard work and contribution to this book, and for making this such a pleasant and wonderful experience. To my photographer, Geoff Dann, and photography assistant, Mark Harvey—it's always so much fun to work with both of you. Thank you all for your expertise in helping to create this book and sharing your individual talents.

This book is dedicated to my beautiful mother with love for passing on all her creative talents! She is a rare gem.